Threads of Imagination

The Collaborative Story of Weaving Worlds

Richard D. Tucci

a DSTL arts publication

Threads of Imagination

The Collaborative Story of Weaving Worlds

a DSTL Arts publication

The work in this book was written by Richard D. Tucci, a participant in DSTL Arts's Poet/Artist Development Program, and first printed in October, 2024 by DSTL Arts publishing in Los Angeles, CA, U.S.A.

Cover Design: Luis Antonio Pichardo

Book Design: Luis Antonio Pichardo

ISBN: 978-1-946081-77-3

10 9 8 7 6 5 4 3 2 1

www.DSTLArts.org

DSTL
arts

Los Angeles, CA

This book is dedicated to myself.

For almost my entire life, I have been told by the people that I cared about most, that I wasn't good enough, and that I didn't deserve to be happy.

So, with this book, and with this dedication, I give myself permission to take up space.

Table of Contents

Why Did I Write This?

The Indian novelist, Savi Sharma, said, that everyone has a story to tell. Everyone is a writer, and while some are written in books, others are confined to hearts. In the end, we always regret the choices we didn't make, the love we didn't accept, and the dreams we didn't fight for.

As for my own story, I grew up in the New York suburbs of Stamford, Connecticut.

Many people see Connecticut as a state of white privilege, and for certain parts, they'd be right. However, my favorite circle of friends were the kids who lived in south Stamford. You see, everything south of the I-95 was low-income housing, and that was where my best friends lived. Once I got my driver's license, I'd sneak out of the house and bring my VHS-C camera; the ones with the little mini-video tapes that would pop out on a spring.

My friend, Tommy, introduced me to the Stamford South Siders, and I'd meet up with them, often late at night, and just record them doing their thing. Sometimes that was trying to get booze from the local liquor store with a fake ID, sometimes that was selling weed on a street corner, and sometimes it was avoiding the cops when they drove through the neighborhood. I wouldn't try to impose my ideas or direct them, I would just let them be themselves and utilize a lot of what I had learned from my Middle Eastern and Jewish family's history of tribal collaborative storytelling. I'd come back home with hours of footage of kids being kids, whether that was loitering, or goofing off in the middle of the street at 1 AM, and then I'd edit it into a short vignette, or a music video.

They. Loved. It! They loved being featured. They loved the music I selected. And when I edited a transition where the camera went through the eye of one of the homeless women and into a new scene with Tommy, THEY FLIPPED THE FUCK OUT!

For that, and other reasons, they watched my back at school, a social environment I didn't exactly thrive in, and they also watched my back when I was filming them, specifically telling me not to come with them down to the docks one night, where I later found out they had a shootout with a rival gang. Nobody got hurt, they just fired guns into the air, and it was more macho posturing than anything, but I was grateful that they wanted to keep me safe.

One of my favorite videos was when Tommy, our friend Don, and I, went to a local sculpture garden and we collectively came up with the story of Don confronting Tommy about his less than legal activities. Then in the story, Don revealed he was actually a supernatural being (like an angel, but cooler), and Tommy followed him into this other realm where all the sculptures were. What I loved about it was how it was surreal and visual like *Alice in Wonderland*. What Tommy loved about it was that it reflected the conflict amongst him and his friends about some of the stuff they did. And what Don loved about it was he got to be the cool center of the story that heralds the conflict.

When I showed Tommy the rough cut, he listened to the hip-hop intro that Don did, basically talking about thug life and gangsta life, but rapping with an excited, lyrical, and rhythmic energy. Tommy hated that intro, saying, "No! It's not—He's like not giving it, it's too

2

exciting. It's like not what the message of it is." Tommy didn't have the words for what he wanted to say, and neither did I, because we were 17. What I learned years later at USC film school was that Don had rapped a verse about this thug life and gangsta life, talking about the negatives, but with an excited energy that made it sound like it was a positive. The medium of how it was presented wound up undermining the message of the short film. This is something filmmakers refer to as *Mise-en-Scène*, where production design, cinematography, and musical arrangement are crafted to support a specific idea.

One other day, I was sitting and talking with Tommy, and I told him about my aspirations of being a filmmaker.

He sheepishly looked at his Nikes, and when I asked what was wrong, he said, "Man, you're gonna go off, and make it big in Hollywood. I can tell. But I ain't never gonna get that. Look at where I live. Who's gonna to take a chance on me? Who's gonna to trust a nigga like me with a million dollars? Why can't I see my stories on the screen?"

I was heartbroken listening to this.

Tommy was my friend, one of the people I trusted the most in the world, but he was never going to get the same joy from seeing his story on the big screen, like I did on a regular basis. Stories are a universal value, a common right that we should all have access to. It shouldn't be restricted, or available to only those who live north of the I-95.

I went off to Hollywood, Tommy went off to be a firefighter, and Don went off to start a fashion line with his name on all the clothes, but I never forgot about that conversation with my best friend.

Over the decades, I've witnessed the means of media production be drastically democratized. Where once you needed a whole studio with camera and lighting equipment, or a book publishing deal, or loads of cash to see your story told, now, you can make a video with your phone, add effects using your phone, upload on your phone, and email the link to all your friends from your phone (this book is not sponsored by "big phone", I swear).

Now, getting people to watch that link is another valid argument, but everyone has the technical ability to tell their story. You can even do primitive CGI with free software like Blender and Unreal Engine.

Also, it's not just film-making, you can self-publish a book for free on Amazon Kindle Direct Publishing. All you need is an internet connection, and the optional Kindle Create software: *https://www.amazon.com/Kindle-Create/*

However, another issue has arisen. Everybody has a story to tell, and everybody has the technical ability to tell their story. However, storytelling is not an innate talent you're born with like some messiah. It's a craft, a muscle that is strengthened over time, and it would be unfair to ask storytellers to take powerful storytelling tools, and expect them to make The Godfather their first time out, or expect them to do it alone. Now that we have democratized storytelling powers, we need to democratize storytelling knowledge.

Too often, people tell their stories, but in a way that can't be understood outside of their inner circle. Trust me, as someone who went to film school, the first screenplay everybody writes is about a teenager who leaves town for Hollywood dreams, but the character has no discernible motivation and is as flat as a saltine.

So, I wanted to see this book as an opportunity to educate, but also to re-imagine storytelling for the 21st century. Over the past twenty years, I've honed these skills in collaborative storytelling to tell my tales, and to empower others to give voice for their own narratives. With this book, I hope you will join me in continuing that tradition of collaborative artistic storytelling.

Character:
Ideas and Concepts Made Into People

Storytelling is a skill, and you have to train and build it up like any other muscle. You can learn it from reading books (ahem) and you can strengthen your stories by continually making things, bringing projects to completion, observing the reaction of your audience, and then making new ones.

There is no secret to what makes a good character.

There's no one magic bullet. Rather, there are several, tiny, little techniques you can employ.

To create a compelling character, you need to decide what kind of story you want to tell. What is your intent?

Odds are, you want your story to have a specific moral or lesson learned. In which case, your character would begin your story believing one thing, and then end the story believing the opposite thing; this change in a character is called a Character Arc. What your character believes at the end is the moral you are trying to impart.

I should be very clear on my stance here. I strongly believe that the best stories are morality plays; and NO, I don't mean Christian morality. I mean the basic principle that a character makes a good choice and is rewarded, while another character makes a bad choice, and is punished. This kind of narrative order allows the audience/us to make sense of the chaos that is life because it is reassuring to us that our own choices will be rewarded, and the choices of those we disagree with will be punished.

One such example is *Scarface*, originally a 1932 film, you're probably most familiar with the 1983 movie starring Al Pacino. The story follows Tony Montana, a Cuban immigrant who escapes to South Florida. His friend, Manny, encourages him to undertake a contract killing, and arranges to get a green card, but he's soon working for drug dealer, Frank Lopez, and brings a new level of violence to Miami. Tony is protective of his younger sister, but his mother knows what he does for a living and disowns him. Tony is impatient and wants it all, including Frank's empire, and even his mistress Elvira Hancock. Once at the top, Tony's outrageous actions make him a target and everything comes crumbling down, leading to his assassination and brutal murder. This clearly shows both a Character Arc and a Morality Play in action, revealing how Tony's character changes externally (by achieving riches beyond his wildest dreams) and also pays a price for his actions.

Heroes and The Dossier Method

The Dossier Method of character creation has been around for several decades, although its exact origin is difficult to pinpoint. It gained popularity among fiction and screenwriters as a structured approach to developing well-rounded and complex characters. It likely emerged in the mid to late 20th century, and over time, the Dossier Method has become a widely recognized and utilized tool in the creative writing process.

In this section, we'll be taking the Dossier Method and heavily modifying it to allow for building your main character with a specific message in mind.

As we stated, your character begins believing the wrong thing and then ends the story believing the correct thing. You can then reverse-engineer your character based on these two values, using the Dossier method.

1. Strength: What is a skill that your character would have that would allow them to succeed? This should be a skill that is inherently neutral, somewhat unique to them, and a skill that would exist whether they believe the right thing OR the wrong thing?

2. Weakness: What is a skill that your character would NOT have that would cause them to fail? This should be a skill that is inherently neutral, somewhat unique to them, and a skill that would NOT be present whether they believe the right thing OR the wrong thing?

3. Flaw: What is a Flaw your character would have, or that another character would point out to them? This flaw should be present in the beginning as they believe the Wrong Thing, but then your character would need to overcome/change this flaw in order to (or as they start to) believe the Right Thing?

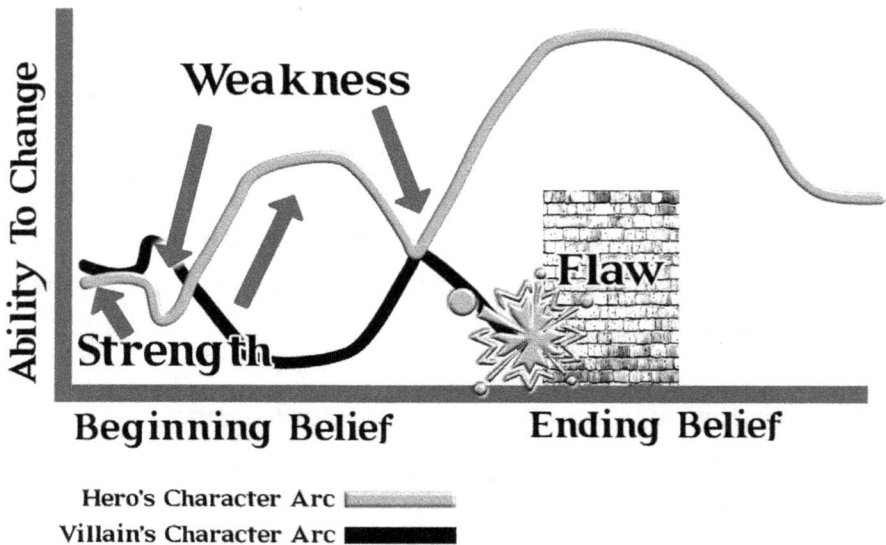

Hero's Character Arc ▭▬▭
Villain's Character Arc ▬▬▬

These core character attributes of a strength, a weakness, and a flaw are invaluable to helping you make your character seem like a real person that an audience will latch onto.

Once you have that, you can ask yourself more questions about who this character is, based on the core values you've created. Note, not all of the answers to these questions need to appear in your story, but it will help you create this character. These questions can also be useful for writing a Persona poem (such as many of the poems of T.S. Elliot), or any activity where you're using a character to consider the nature of humanity.

4. How old are they?

5. What kind of education did they receive?

6. What was their favorite topic in school? And their least favorite topic in school?

7. What body part have they always felt insecure about?

8. What do they think about religion and God?

9. What is their favorite time of day?

10. What is their favorite season?

11. Do they have a lucky number? And if so, what is it?

12. Where did they grow up? Where did they want to grow up? What socioeconomic class did your character grow up in?

13. Where are they now?

14. Where are they going?

15. Do they prefer watching sunrises or sunsets?

16. What kind of furniture do they have in their home?

17. What kind of people do they gravitate towards?

18. Who was their best friend?

19. Were they bullied or were they a bully when they were younger?

20. Do they have a good luck charm? If so, what is it?

21. What does your character want?

22. What kind of obstacles does the character create for themselves (we all do)?

23. What does the character do when they meet an obstacle?

24. Does the character solve problems with their brains, or their brawns?

25. What's the thing they've always longed for that they've never been able to grasp?

Let's look at how this applies to Neo from *The Matrix*; I like this example because Lana and Lilly Wachowski did us the favor of placing Neo's character arc in the dialogue, as long as you know where to look.

Neo begins the film believing that the rules which exist are unchangeable, and does not believe in himself. He's more focused on the boundaries of what he can't do rather than the possibilities of what he wants to do. His supervisor even drills this in by threatening to fire Neo if he doesn't conform to what is expected of him.

Neo's flaw is also tied to his opening belief since it is holding him back. We can see in the film that he never leaves the apartment, he initially doesn't want to go out to the nightclub with his client, and he's also afraid of the cops tracking the data back to him.

Neo's strength is that he is a gifted hacker and quick-witted, with Morpheus complimenting, good. Adaptation. Improvisation. But your weakness isn't your technique. Or at least he said something very close to that; I can't give you the exact quote due to copyright law.

Neo's weakness is something much simpler than his flaw; whereas his flaw is a fear of the rules catching up with him, his weakness is his own self-doubt, which does not go away in the character arc of the first film, but we see his self-doubt persist throughout the other films as well.

Neo ends the film believing that anything is possible, and there's actually a great line in the screenplay that was chopped up in the final film, "When I used to look out at this world, all I could see was its edges, its boundaries, its rules and controls, its leaders and laws. But now, I see another world. A different world where all things are possible. A world of hope. Of peace."

Exceptions

There are many characters in classic and popular media that are too small or appear for too short of a time to have a worthwhile character arc, and this is fine. While it would be great if every character in your story had an arc, it's not a requirement.

Some of you might say that not all stories need character arcs. This is also true, sometimes we just enjoy reading/watching a character because they're just cool, and good at what they do. Some of the most popular characters in culture have no character arc and are considered iconic characters, like Indiana Jones, James Bond, and Winnie The Pooh.

With these kind of iconic characters, they may not change, but they often inspire changes in others. We can see this going back to classic fables, such as *The Pied Piper of Hamelin*. In that classic fable, the Piper's magical ability to lead away the town's rats (and later its children) doesn't change throughout the story. However, his actions inspire change in the townspeople, who must face the consequences of their broken promises and learn the importance of honoring their commitments. We can also see this in many famous comic book characters, in something Stan Lee labeled, "The Illusion of Change" where characters like Peter Parker will go from high school to college. He'll get a new girlfriend or marry, he'll get a new nemesis, he'll save countless people's lives through his heroic and inspirational actions, but at his core, he still remains the same character with the same problems of balancing great power and great responsibility.

When looking at your story, your own talents/preferences, and the moral you want to tell, you need to ask what kind of character works best for this story.

Villains

I'm of the opinion that the best stories come out when characters represent an ideal or a philosophy. For example, in the film, *The Dark Knight*, Batman/Bruce Wayne represents the idea that people are inherently good and worth saving, while The Joker (and by extension, Two-Face) represents the idea that people and times are inherently evil, and being a decent person is not only futile, but impossible. However, rather than engaging in long monologues, these characters show us their motivations through their actions.

We also see this in their character arcs, where Bruce Wayne sacrifices his Batman persona, ending with the belief that Harvey Dent first espoused, that you either die a hero, or live long enough

12

to see yourself become a villain. Meanwhile, the Joker does not change, he is the same at the beginning compared to the end.

The villain not only embodies what your character believes in at the beginning of their journey but also serves as a shadowy reflection of your hero.

Conclusion

Rather than summarizing all the points previously discussed, I'd like to try and simplify all this. In an interview, Francis Ford Coppola said, "When I'm making a movie, I boil the core theme down to a single word, and that word motivates every decision that I have to make. When directing *The Conversation*, that one word theme was privacy, and that's what motivated all my decisions, like the decision to put Harry Kaul [Gene Hackman's character] in a see-through raincoat for the whole film."

Author Kurt Vonnegut did something similar, placing an index card with the book's message on it above his desk, filtering all his writing decisions through that message. That is what our Dossier Method is meant to do, help us focus on our characters through the focusing lens of a clear message, because in the end, people don't care about speeches and grand pronouncements. People care about other people, and if you want to move someone, make them care about another person.

Writing Exercise:

Identify a core belief you have and want others to share. Now, create a character, as well as their character arc, for the story based on the method we've outlined above.

_____

_____

_____

_____

_____

_____

_____

_____

_____

_____

_____

_____

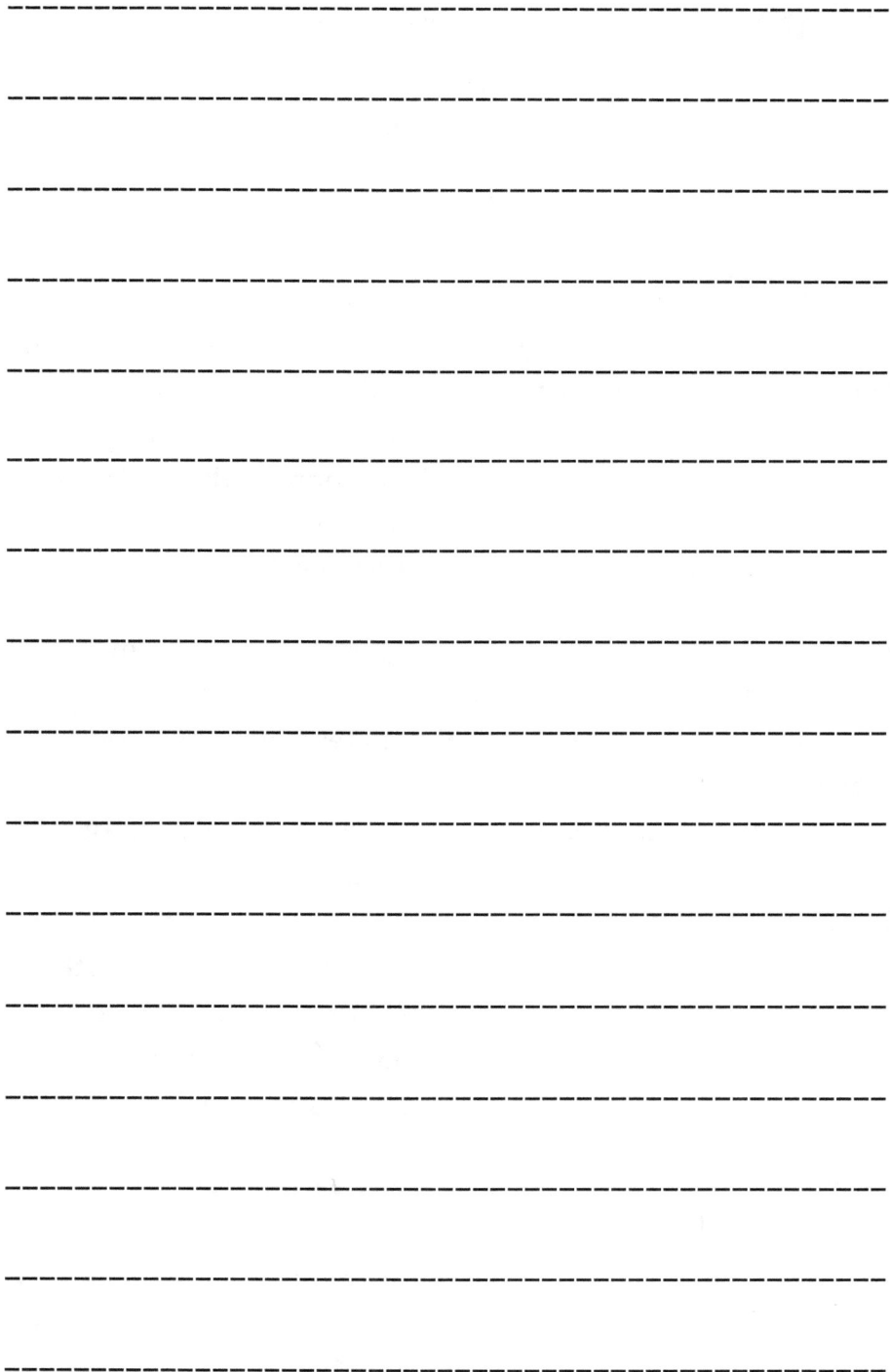

Conflict:
Relationships Between Characters that Contrast Ideologies

I think it's safe to say I grew up in a troubled home, and while we never went to bed hungry, it was often cold, frightening, and sometimes dangerous. One memory that stands out is the time my mom tried to run over my dad with her car, and I was in the car at the time. As a result, I've always had trouble relating to characters in stories who had strong relationships with their parents; I immediately check out as a result.

Conversely, I was blessed with many great teachers and mentors, both virtually, via educational television, and in person. Teachers who cared about me like my AP History teacher, Ms. Gibson, who would try to comfort me when I went into a downward spiral of anxiety, and Mrs. Seagull who just wanted to help a kid dealing with a difficult home life. I was also able to survive that environment because of educational children's programs that showed me there was a wider world outside my home. I ate up everything from *Fraggle Rock* to *Donald Duck Goes to Mathemagic Land* (yes, that's a real program), to even *The World of David the Gnome* which covered nature lessons in its fantasy narrative.

Now, I want to create that kind of show for kids, like me, growing up in a difficult environment. As a result, I am attracted to stories that are educational or deal with mentors in some capacity, because I find empathy and comfort in those relationships, including *Fight Club*, *Finding Forrester*, *Get Shorty*, and others.

However, I digress, this book is about storytelling, so how can we use these relationship connections to engage our audience?

Well, remember that chart we had? The one that looks like it was drawn with crayons by a five year old? In that chart, we show the hero's character arc is inherently tied to the villain's character arc because our human brain defines concepts in relationship to one another. It's a limitation of how we learn, but also explains why you often describe new friends by their relationships to old ones, like Chuck's new girlfriend, or Melissa's new drug dealer.

Furthermore, it's a big part of why we define stories with conflict, and we classify stories by the type of conflict:

- Person vs. Person
- Person vs. Nature
- Person vs. Society
- Person vs. Technology
- Person vs. Supernatural
- Person vs. Self
- Person vs. Destiny (Fate/Luck/God)

Then there are the lesser known forms of conflict:

- Person vs. Social Media
- Person vs. Their Mother In Law
- Person vs. A Post-Apocalyptic Warlord
- Person vs. A Japanese Ghost
- Person vs. A Creepy Doll
- Person vs. A Non-Fiction Author Who Turns Everything Into A Joke

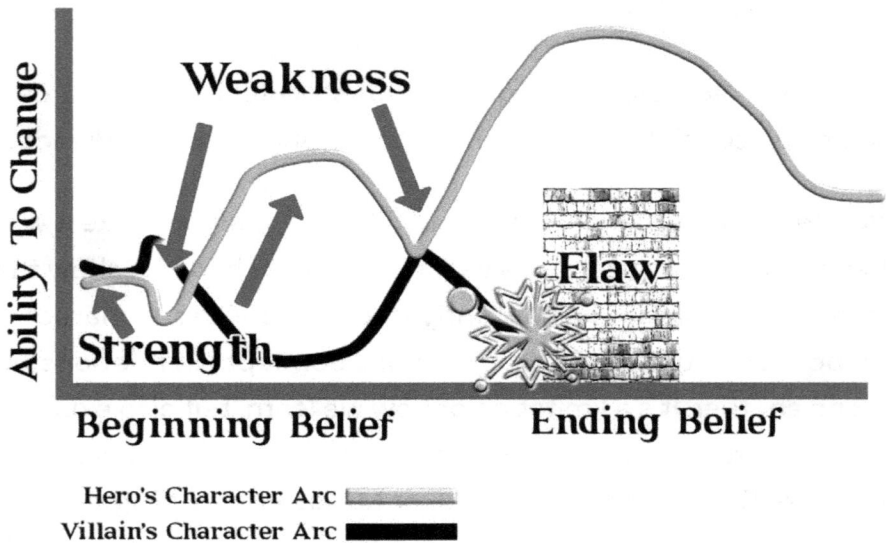

Ability To Change

Weakness

Strength

Flaw

Beginning Belief

Ending Belief

Hero's Character Arc
Villain's Character Arc

However, if you think about your favorite stories, odds are there's a personal connection between the Hero, the Antagonist, and the other characters. There's a reason for this, and it is authenticity.

At the core of storytelling lies the belief that authenticity breeds the best tales. Truthful characters, basic relationships, and clear objectives form the bedrock of compelling narratives. By basing the story around relationships, we can create genuine reactions and engagement from the audience, rather than through contrived plot twists. It's an old piece of advice to write what you know, and we all know about interpersonal relationships, whether it's your romantic partner, your best friend, or your next-door neighbor/rival. One of the six core principles of storytelling is to focus on relationships between partners, but we'll get to those core principles later.

The relationships portrayed within a story are crucial for giving characters depth and resonance. Conflict between two strangers pales in comparison to the tension between individuals who share a history. When characters are connected, the audience is more likely to empathize with their struggles and triumphs. Take, for example, the story of Romulus and Remus.

Romulus and Remus were brothers who shared a love for one another, who survived the harsh Italian woods by being suckled by a she-wolf, and were adopted by a local shepherd. The brothers grew up to become natural-born leaders, and went off to form their own city. The two disagreed on who would lead the city, what it would be named, and even which of the 7 hills it should be built on. After Romulus was found to be favored by the Gods by a sign of having birds flying around him, he was determined to be the ruler. Shortly thereafter, Remus was killed by Romulus for challenging his rule.

This story of familial love, sibling rivalry, and then brotherly fratricide not only engages us through the emotional conflict of the two, but would later define the shifting power struggles in the Roman empire, including Caesar, Nero, Augustus, and the frequent assassinations that would occur.

One can apply this to almost any story. I think it's a pretty safe bet that you (yes, YOU) will never be the Pharaoh of Egypt, or grow up in the Egyptian royal court, so it's going to be hard for you to connect with people in that setting. However, consider the rivalry between Moses and Ramses in ancient Egypt.

While few of us can relate to the grandeur of pharaohs and royal courts, sibling rivalry is a universal experience. By anchoring the story in a common relationship, such as the bond between brothers, storytellers can tap into the audience's empathy and create narratives that resonate across cultures and time periods.

Relationships between characters serve as a powerful lens

through which storytellers convey their values, foster empathy, and build communal connections. One of the key insights I've gleaned from the storytelling practices of Jewish and Turkish itinerant tribes is the importance of relationships in conveying cultural values and fostering empathy.

Characters in these narratives served as vessels for transmitting moral lessons, social norms, and communal values, inviting audiences to empathize with their struggles and triumphs. Through the shared experience of storytelling, listeners gained a deeper understanding of the storytellers' worldview and forged connections across cultural boundaries. The relationships between characters in a story serve as a powerful vehicle for conveying the values of the storyteller(s) and fostering empathy and communal connections.

While the storyteller can create any relationship dynamic they want for characters and their conflicting ideologies, if we review some examples even deeper, then we see common themes in specific relationship types.

Family Relationships (Capitalism)

In the folktale, *The Pied Piper of Hamelin*, the villagers lose their children after betraying their promise to the Pied Piper, establishing the lesson that if you go back on your word, you'll lose what is most dear to you.

In the film, *Scarface*, Tony Montana doesn't team up with a group of random thugs. His right-hand man is his friend from childhood, Manny, and Manny's perceived betrayal of sleeping with Tony's sister Gina results in his death, showing how the corruption of drugs and cocaine can cause an Oedipal-like sin.

In the film, *The Godfather*, Michael Corleone isn't struggling against strangers, he's dealing with the conflict and turmoil within his own family. He struggles to overcome the corruption that defines his clan, but winds up being sucked into it through the violence against them, and the need to defend them. In fact, Francis Ford Coppola intended for *The Godfather* to be an allegory about capitalism, and how "the family business" can wind up destroying something pure.

In the 1990 play written by Josefina López, *Real Women Have Curves*, Ana Garcia is not fighting against banks or any symbol of institutional racism, but against her own mother because of her desire to keep Ana at home and help provide for the family. This conflict between mother and daughter establishes a conflict between an old way of thinking, and a new way of thinking (old guard vs. new guard), while also addressing the same capitalist themes from *The Godfather*.

Family-Adjacent Relationships (Revenge)

In the movie *Star Wars: A New Hope*, Luke meets Obi-Wan Kenobi and quickly forms a bond with him when he discovers that he fought with his father in the Clone Wars, including being told that Darth Vader killed his father. This news (along with the death of his uncle and aunt) propel his journey against the empire. When Luke discovers that Darth Vader is actually his father, it grounds the story as a dramatic family saga against an impossible-to-comprehend backdrop of a galactic civil war.

In the *Harry Potter* book series, Harry knows Voldemort because Voldemort killed his parents, setting a chain of events in motion, leading to Harry's powerful status in the wizarding world, but also makes Harry's struggle to defeat Voldemort a proper revenge story, which many audience members can relate to, as they feel an empathy behind the idea of lost parents.

In the movie *Pirates of the Caribbean: The Curse of the Black Pearl*, Will Taylor desperately loves Elizabeth Swan and goes out to rescue her when she is kidnapped. To add to the story, Jack Sparrow knew Will's father, Bootstrap Bill when he was still alive, but hesitantly shares this information, establishing the story as a murky mixture of loyalties and connections. This adds to the drama by never letting the audience know who will do what.

Friendship Relationships (Overcoming Adversity)

In most *Winnie the Pooh* books, Pooh knows Tigger, Eeyore, and Christopher Robin because they are all friends, establishing the story with the premise that friendship and caring for one another is the most important virtue of all.

In the book series, *The Adventures Of Sherlock Holmes*, the friendship between Sherlock and John Watson is one of the most iconic and enduring relationships in literature. Despite their differences in temperament and approach, they form a complementary partnership that transcends mere companionship, and allows the reader to understand the difference between them, since we all have that one friend we butt heads with but also admire. Their bond is forged through countless adventures, trials, and shared experiences, demonstrating unwavering trust, mutual respect, and genuine affection.

Rivalry Relationships (Danger)

In the film *Raiders of The Lost Ark*, Indiana Jones knows virtually everybody on some deeper level, including the villain, Belloq, as the two of them are competitors for priceless artifacts, with Belloq willing to steal items for the highest bidder, even Adolf Hitler. The juxtaposition of the two even highlights the danger of Indiana Jones falling to the dark side, with Belloq saying the old trope line that he and Indiana are very much alike. Archaeology is their religion, yet they have both fallen from the purer faith. Their methods have not differed as much as Indiana pretends. Belloq is a shadowy reflection of Indy. It would take only a nudge to make Indy like him and to push him out of the light. Indiana also knows Marion Ravenwood, who has the Medallion leading to the lost Ark, because they previously had a romantic relationship, establishing that Indiana not only needs to save the world from the Nazis but also save the woman he loves from those who wish to do harm, at all costs.

In *Batman* comic books, The Joker is not a random street thug, but has a sick obsession with Batman, constantly desiring to be his one and only nemesis. This rivalry and obsession underscores the theme of duality and the fine line between heroism and villainy, as both characters are defined by their opposition to one another.

In Francis Ford Coppola's film *The Conversation*, Harry Kaul knows the villains as paid clients who seek his expertise in surveillance, but Harry develops a sense of paranoia and fear around them and the work they ask him to do, underscoring the film's exploration of morality, guilt, and the complexities of surveillance.

Relationships of Admiration (Savior)

In the film, *The Matrix*, Neo isn't picked off the street by a stranger, he's contacted by a pair of hackers whom he knows of by reputation, and even admires, saying it's an honor to meet Morpheus and Trinity when he first greets them. This establishes the story as a journey into an uncharted and honorable frontier of saving humanity.

In most *Spider-Man* comic books, Peter Parker knows his nemeses, at one time looking up to them as heroes, such as Dr. Otto Octavius (Doc Ock), Norman Osborn (Green Goblin), Ned Leeds (Hobgoblin), Harry Osborn (New Goblin), Dr. Curtis Connors (Lizard), etc. This reflects the idea that even those closest to us can become adversaries, whether due to personal conflicts, external manipulation, or their own descent into darkness, and it mimics how we often feel betrayed by our heroes and friends as we grow older and learn how complex the world really is.

In the movie *Casablanca*, Rick admires Victor Laszlo because of his anti-fascist reputation, but he knows Ilsa Lund through their brief but passionate romance in Paris, establishing the story as a battle between love and virtue.

In the TNT show, *Snowpiercer*, Andre Layton develops a kinship with the Tailies (stowaways who live in the Tail of the Mighty Train, the last remaining habitat for humans on Earth). That camaraderie is depicted through a handful of specific relationships, including

Andre's respect for Old Ivan. When Old Ivan dies, it shows how important the Snowpiercer rebellion is to both Ivan and Andre, and how Andre must save the last remnants of humanity.

The Gods
(Omnipresent Relationships)

In the various books of The Torah (the Hebrew Bible), God is portrayed as the father of all the beings on Earth. This relationship of connecting God to all the animals, the trees, the first humans, AND the people in the individual stories creates an inherent connection between A) the religious forces depicted, B) the specific character in that story, and C) the reader. It's a rather direct way of creating a story that has an omnipresent relationship with the reader that isn't available in most other conflicts.

Similarly, in most Ancient Greek legends, Zeus was connected to almost every story and every character through his prodigious... pursuit of women characters. Because of this, Zeus felt connected to the specific character in that story, as well as the reader, again involving the reader as part of the story.

Think about it, if a character you're reading about is connected to a God, and that God is connected to real world elements that you worship, then the story of that character is going to have extra impact on you, as you see an A to B to C relationship by proxy.

In the Biblical story of Christ, Jesus is not betrayed by a stranger, he is betrayed by his closest follower, Judas, who knows him well. This familiarity paints Judas' betrayal as a necessary step in fulfilling the prophecy of Jesus' crucifixion and subsequent resurrection, which in biblical canon absolves humans of original sin. This connection between God, Jesus, Judas, and original sin highlights the idea of God's sovereignty and ultimate control over human events.

Conclusion

In conclusion, relationships between characters are the backbone of compelling storytelling, serving as a powerful lens through which storytellers convey their values, foster empathy, and build connections with their audience. They allow audiences to empathize with characters' struggles and triumphs, fostering a shared understanding and communal connection.

By focusing on authentic, relatable relationships, storytellers can create narratives that not only entertain but also convey profound lessons and values. Whether through the bonds of family, the camaraderie of friends, the tension of rivals, or the reverence for mentors, these relationships provide a rich tapestry for exploring the human condition and its myriad complexities.

Writing Exercise:

As we craft our own stories, let us remember the power of these connections. Using the examples above, identify the relationship between your hero and your villain that draws out the most emotional reaction, while also conveying the type of conflict between ideologies you want to demonstrate. THEN use the Dossier method in the previous section to write out who your antagonist is in relation to your hero.

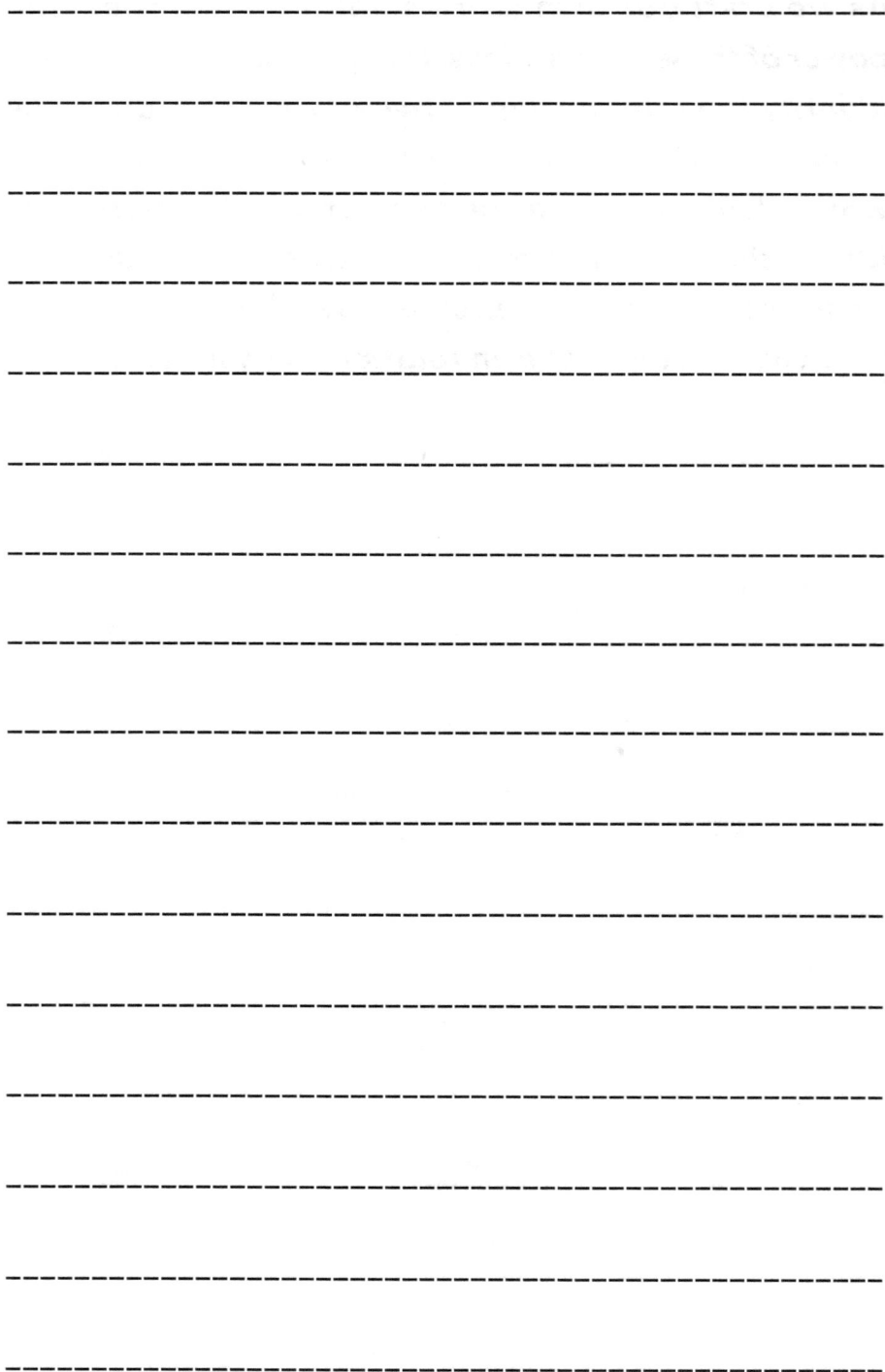

Need some help? Here are the Dossier questions you can ask to decide who your villain is.

- How old are they?
- What kind of education did they receive?
- What were their favorite and least favorite topics in school?
- What body part have they always felt insecure about?
- What do they think about religion and God?
- What is their favorite time of day?
- What is their favorite season?
- Do they have a lucky number? And if so, what is it?
- Where did they grow up? Where did they want to grow up? What socioeconomic class did your character grow up in?
- Where are they now?
- Where are they going?
- Do they prefer watching sunrises or sunsets?
- What kind of furniture do they have in their home?
- What kind of people do they gravitate towards?
- Who was their best friend?
- Were they bullied or were they a bully when they were younger?
- Do they have a good luck charm? If so, what is it?
- What does your character want?
- What kind of obstacles does the character create for themselves (we all do)?
- What does the character do when they meet an obstacle?
- Does the character solve problems with their brains, or their brawns?
- What's the thing they've always longed for that they've never been able to grasp?

The Audience is Also The Storyteller

There's a pernicious belief that art, history, literature, and society only advance through the actions of great men, which posits that certain exceptional storytellers hold sway over the evolution of their craft. This is called *The Great Man Theory*, and these men (and yes, they are usually WHITE men in this colonialist view of art) have a decisive historical effect because they are born "special" with superior intellect, heroic courage, extraordinary leadership abilities, or divine inspiration.

As a multiracial Jew living with an invisible disability, I have some serious problems with this, because it is based on the idea that some people are born special, and that REALLY doesn't sit well with me, since that logic has been used to justify eugenics, subjugation, slavery, and genocide, not to mention grave robbing, such as when Albert Einstein's brain was robbed from his body and dissected against his wishes.

As Stephen Jay Gould wrote in *The Panda's Thumb*, he was less interested in the weight and convolutions of Einstein's brain than in the near certainty that people of equal talent have lived and died in cotton fields and sweatshops. *The Great Man Theory* perspective neglects the influence of broader social and cultural dynamics, such as Social Justice movements, popular art movements, or marches towards other progressive values, but admittedly, that's a bit abstract. Let's get into the nitty-gritty.

In practical terms, storytellers have always maintained connections with their audiences and communities. From ancient itinerant tribes to modern collaborative techniques (like long-form improv) storytelling has never been a solitary endeavor. We draw inspiration from collective experiences and interactions, shaping our narratives based on the feedback and engagement of those around us. By acknowledging the collaborative nature of storytelling, we can create more immersive and engaging narratives that resonate with diverse audiences, because (believe it or not) the collective power of live storytelling is more powerful, entertaining, and accurate than the trope of a solitary, tortured artist.

The Science

Francis Galton was a British statistician, and in 1906, he visited a livestock fair where an ox was on display and the villagers were invited to guess the animal's weight. Afterwards, Galton asked for the tickets that people had written their guesses on, and he thought that there may be a few individual guesses that were close, while the group average would be far off. To his astonishment, all the individual guesses were wide off, but the group average was less than 1% different from the actual weight. This was the beginning of what's referred to as *Standard Deviation*, which is an important mathematical concept about the grouping of data.

However, this is one of many examples of group work being better than the work of any one individual. When groups work better than we would expect, given the individuals who form them, we call the outcome a process gain. This can even be written out mathematically, and we can write the following equation to express this relationship:

potential productivity
– process loss
+ process gain
_____
actual productivity

I know, there's nothing that gets you more excited than math, but now we get into why it matters.

Ancient Collaboration

From my own background of the itinerant tribes of Jewish and Turkish descent, their nomadic lifestyle required storytelling as a means of connection and survival. While roaming through the Middle East and Eastern Europe, these tribes relied on storytelling to earn the trust of locals and navigate unfamiliar territories. Stories were shared through various mediums, from one-on-one fortune-telling to communal gatherings around fires, blending tribal narratives with local customs and legends.

While the traveling storytellers knew the framework of their stories, they would NOT have every word memorized. In fact, it was quite common for storytellers to modify and update their stories for each local village they passed through and would often determine these modifications based on feedback from the local audiences in the form of gasps, laughter, and tears. This is especially true when a storyteller is performing in theater of the mind, be it around a campfire or a black box stage, where the world must be imagined by the audience.

One of the ways they accomplished this was by having set

archetypes and structures for stories, with specific segments cut out for local flavor to be added.

For example, one of the folkloric creatures they would tell stories about were the Mullo, an undead revenant described as having white clothes, hair that reaches to their feet, and one physical oddity (a trait which varies from geographic region to region). Anyone who had a horrible appearance, was missing a finger, or had appendages similar to those of an animal, was believed to be a mullo.

A mullo's purpose was to seek out people it disliked in life and to harass that person, which included family members, and returning to the Earthly realm to commit malicious acts like attacking by strangling and sucking the blood of a person. To ward off mullos, Romani people drove steel or iron needles into a corpse's heart and placed bits of steel in the mouth, over the eyes, ears, and between the fingers at the time of burial.

In India, where the Romani people originated, similar tales of Vetalas, ghoul-like beings that inhabit corpses, are found in old Sanskrit folklore. The vetalas are described as creatures who, like the bat, hang upside down on trees found on cremation grounds and cemeteries.

In ancient Hebrew cultures in the Middle East, there was the Alukah (the literal translation of 'leech') which is synonymous with the term Motetz Dam (literally, 'bloodsucker'). The creature is understood to be a living human being, but can shape-shift into a wolf, and would eventually die if prevented from feeding on blood for a long enough time. The alukah can also fly by releasing its long hair, an allusion to kabbalistic teachings that Jews should allow their hair to grow long in Payot or Payos, stretching back to the Dead Sea

Scrolls, and continuing to Orthodox Jewish communities today. I want to make clear, this was not a creature meant to slander the Jews, but was a creature believed by Middle Eastern Jews to exist.

In Turkic Europe, two of the earliest historical recordings of similar creatures can be found in *Neplach's Chronicle*, probably written in 1360 which directly correlates to when Sinti and Roma people began moving into Europe. For the year 1336, Neplach (the historian) mentions a shepherd named Myslata from Blov. He died and was buried, but he didn't stay in the grave. Each evening, Myslata walked around, spoke to people as if alive, and scared them. Soon, he started killing people, and if he stopped by someone's home and called their name, said person would die in eight days. So the people of several villages decided to exhume him and burn his body. During the process, Myslata let out a loud scream.

In the Dalmatian region of Croatia, there is a female creature called a Mora, or Morana, who drinks the blood of men, and also the kuzlac/kozlak, the recently-dead who have not lived piously. They can be men or women who show themselves at crossroads, bridges, caves, and graveyards and frighten the locals by terrorizing their homes and drinking their blood. To be killed, a wooden stake must be thrust through them.

In Romania, these creatures were first called "Moroi" (from the Romanian word mort meaning "dead" or the Slavic word meaning "nightmare") and then later renamed to "Strigoi". Similarly, dead strigoi were described as reanimated corpses that also sucked blood and attacked their living family. Live strigoi became revenants after their death. A person born with a caul, an extra (oddity) nipple, a tail, or extra hair was doomed to become a strigoi.

In Croatia, Slovenia, the Czech Republic, and Slovakia, a creature called Pijavica, which literally translates to 'leech', is used to describe a creature who has led an evil and sinful life as a human and, in turn, becomes a powerfully strong, cold-blooded killer. Its former family can only protect their homes by placing mashed garlic and wine at their windows and thresholds to keep it from entering. It can only be killed by fire while awake and by using the Rite of Exorcism if found in its grave during the day.

By now, you can recognize this creature as the prototype of a Vampire. While many speculate that these proto-vampires arose simultaneously, I would argue that the archetypes for these creatures existed in India circa 700 CE, and through the itinerant communities' use of collaborative storytelling, perpetuated and adapted to local cultures, thus giving us the modern-day vampire.

Basically, without the itinerant storytellers changing and evolving their stories through collaborative practices and feedback from the live audience, you don't get Dracula.

Today, itinerant tribes continue to face persecution, underscoring the ongoing relevance of storytelling as a tool for resilience and resistance. Their stories remind us of the enduring power of storyteller-audience relationships in shaping our understanding of the world and connecting us across diverse communities and experiences. As storytellers, we inherit a rich tapestry of narratives, woven together by the threads of history, culture, and human connection.

Modern Collaboration

Collaborative storytelling in the 21st century has undergone a transformation thanks to the vast capabilities of technology.

Gone are the days of solitary confinement for storytellers, locked away in their abodes, hoping for a compelling finished product. Instead, modern creators have a myriad of options for collaborating with fellow storytellers and engaging with diverse audiences.

Online platforms, such as blogs and forums, provide writers with a space to share their work and receive feedback from a wide range of readers. However, navigating online spaces can be tricky, as negative comments and destructive-criticism are often prevalent. A better example of collaborative storytelling might be long-form improvisation.

Long-form improvisation has a surprising and hidden legacy. Improvisational storytelling, as we know it today, began in Chicago's Near West Side at the convergence of several poor, immigrant neighborhoods. First-generation Russian-Jew Viola Spolin was NOT an actress or a writer, she was a social worker. Growing up in depression-era Chicago, she trained under sociologist, Neva Boyd, at Hull House in Chicago, a settlement house and community center for immigrants. Hull House had English and Citizenship classes, as well as job training to help uplift the poor via education. The Chicago Park Commission hired Boyd as a social worker, specifically to organize social clubs, direct dramatics, and supervise social dances and play activities, but Boyd believed that art and cultural activities were just as important to the learning experience, and so she hired Viola Spolin to help run the program.

Viola was a walking encyclopedia and could memorize every game, rule set, and artistic challenge that the children played in an effort to show how play could assist with learning, confidence, and social skills. When Boyd was hired by FDR's

Works Progress Administration, she made sure Spolin was chosen as drama supervisor for the Chicago branch of the Works Progress Administration's Recreational Project.

Boyd and Spolin came from completely different backgrounds, Spolin being the child of Jewish immigrants growing up in the big city slums, while Boyd grew up on a farm in Iowa amongst conservative Christian parents. However, they both saw a clear need to create an easily grasped system of theater training and storytelling that could cross the cultural and ethnic barriers of the immigrant children with whom they worked.

Viola did this by creating a set of theater games, including *Gibberish Interpreter*, *Mirror*, *Spacewalk*, and others that are still in use today. These simple, short-form children's games are literally the birth of American improvisation, and Spolin went on to form an actor's company and school where she would train actors at Second City Chicago, including Alan Arkin, Joan Rivers, Peter Boyle, John Belushi, John Candy, Bill Murray, Dan Aykroyd, Eugene Levy, Gilda Radner, Del Close, and many, many others.

One of her Chicago students, Del Close, would go on to pioneer the long-form improv game called, *The Harold*, where improvisers would take turns telling a long-form story with character arcs and narrative structure, teaching students like Amy Poehler, Vince Vaughn, Bob Odenkirk, Tina Fey, and many more.

Whereas Spolin's work was based around improv games that were two or three minutes long, Close's *Harold* would have an improviser team telling a coherent story over 30 to 60 minutes.

Close later teamed up with Charna Halpern and Kim "Howard" Johnson to write the 1994 book *Truth in Comedy* which discusses the long-form improv formats, such as *The Harold*. The principles of this book include:

- Be honest in the scene and be in the moment
- Strive to make your scene partner look good
- No idea is a bad idea, make active choices
- Listen to your scene partner
- Create an environment on stage
- Focus on relationships between partners

How Does This Impact Satire and Authority

From the archetypal characters that the audience is familiar with, one can then use the understanding of these power dynamics to craft a story that will engage audiences. While traditional storytelling often assigns authority to protagonists, mentors, or narrators, collaborative and improvisational formats challenge these conventions, thereby allowing for a more fluid distribution of influence.

In such formats, authority can manifest in various forms, ranging from the commanding presence of a storyteller to the collective power of an ensemble cast. In other words, it's not the size of your cast, it's how you use it.

One aspect of authority in collaborative storytelling is its relationship with satire. Satire, with its penchant for subversion and critique, often targets figures of authority, challenging their legitimacy and exposing their flaws. In collaborative settings, creators have the opportunity to wield satire as a tool for social commentary, using humor and irony to question established power structures and provoke thought.

However, the effectiveness of satire hinges on the audience's perception of authority. A character or narrative deemed authoritative may be more resistant to satire, as the audience's investment in their credibility may hinder their willingness to question or critique that character. Conversely, challenging authority figures or conventions can be a potent source of comedic and narrative tension, inviting audiences to reconsider their assumptions and perspectives. From the wise mentor archetype to the tyrannical ruler, archetypal characters embody familiar roles and traits that resonate with audiences on a subconscious level. This kind of collaborative group-think helps embolden a storyteller to go further faster with their narratives.

However, the most compelling stories often subvert or complicate traditional archetypes, offering fresh perspectives and challenging entrenched narratives. Just take a look at Brandon Sanderson's *The Hope of Elantris* where he subverted an archetype, and branded the story as more original simply by making the wise old mentor character a woman instead of a man, which had rarely (if ever) been done before.

In collaborative and improvisational storytelling, creators have the freedom to experiment with archetypal roles, infusing their characters with complexity, nuance, and unexpected twists. Because the storyteller(s) are at the center of the stage, they are immediately given authority in creating their world, and thus should use it to advance their own ideas and values.

Writing Exercise:

Create a world of speculative fiction (in a genre of sci-fi, fantasy, horror, ya know, the fun genres). In creating this world, think about the things that give it life: cities; creatures; traditions; anything that makes it unique from our world. Now, identify the places where your fellow storytellers could provide detail and color about how that world works?

Story Structure

It was a dark, quiet room in the University of Southern California film school. People often assumed that USC was an affluent campus filled with expensive equipment and privilege. However, there were still some corners, like the School of Cinema and Television's Lucas instructional building (yes, that Lucas) that had a subtle smell of mildew from its 30 years of a busy and sun-avoidant student body.

About a dozen of us sat there, anxiously awaiting our professor of two weeks, Academy Award winning writer, Seth Winston. We originally thought the 8am class would not be an issue, given we had just left a high-school career where we had 7 AM classes every day. Boy were we wrong.

In walked Winston, equally tired and carrying a tennis bag. After a brief intro, he invited us to read the first few pages of Act 1 of our short script. He listened attentively, and as he began to critique the first student, he reached into his tennis bag and pulled out a bottle of Johnny Walker Green and poured it into his "I hate Mondays" coffee mug.

After his critique, one of my fellow film students (who later abandoned Hollywood and became a criminal defense attorney) asked about the bottle of Johnny Walker, to which Winston replied, "Oh yeah, I guess I should hide this, in case an administrator walks in."

He then turned to me, and I read the first few pages of my short—a romantic comedy where a woman who is a vampire falls in love with a mortal, and has to come out to him with the truth.

After contemplatively listening with his finger to his chin, Winston turned to me and said, "Why do I care?"

"I—What?"

"Why do I care about this person? Why do I care about her loving this guy? Why do I care about whether she dates him or eats him? Why do I care?"

I was dumbfounded and had no response.

"You gotta understand, the best movies are the most important moment of a person's life. It is the story that defined them and formed their identity. Hell! A story IS life. A movie IS life, just with the boring parts cut out, and at the end of that story, our protagonist must change in a fundamental way, because ALL of us in the audience, go through moments where we change in a fundamental way."

So, why is story structure important to making an audience care about your story?

Well, let's start with the acknowledgment that many people don't like story structure. They say the rules are contrived and the barriers are artificial, forcing writers to retell the same story over and over again.

The critics of story structure say that adhering to any structure, even as simple as a 3-act structure (which has been around since ancient Greece), prevents experimentation and progress in narrative forms.

Now, I would be willing to concede that genre rules can place a burden on writers, placing stagnant formats and requirements on storytellers, telling them to add an action scene on page 15, and a sex scene on page 55.

However, if we decouple genre from story structure, we can see that story structure provides just that: structure.

It prevents us from languishing in the self-aggrandizing and masturbatory sub plots. It helps keep us focused on what the audience (be it reader, watcher, or game player) cares about most: our character(s) and their struggles.

In this book, we're going to delve into a story structure that I believe is essential, because it emulates how the human mind thinks and organizes its way through life.

This is especially important in collaborative storytelling because, once all the storytellers understand the bones of the structure, it gives everyone more freedom to hang interesting elements of that story off of that structure, because the human mind will recognize these vital story beats.

The Science

Humanity has long acknowledged its link to gorillas, monkeys, and other primates. Since Darwin, we have observed these creatures in their natural habitats, and seen the similarities they have with us, from opposable thumbs to their care-giving groups.

According to DNA sequencing, there's only 4% difference in the genomes that make up ours and their DNA. Hundreds of in-depth studies around the world have been performed to try and tell the differences between primates and humans. A European study found that a key difference between primates and humans is our recognition of time.

The study indicated that primates reset their clocks after each time interval during tasks, relying on the association between elapsed time and target position in physical space. Researchers speculate that the spatial aspect of the task helped monkeys perceive and maintain rhythms of different paces.

Do you understand what I'm talking about? No? I don't blame you. Let me give you the simpler version.

Primates witness patterns, but cannot think about time in the same abstract way as humans (hours, days, seasons, years, etc.).

This may seem like a small thing, but you have so many building blocks of storytelling in the abstract box of time: changes in the season; physical growth with changes in age; mental and emotional changes; and the very concept of cause and effect.

Every story is about how one thing led to another, whether intentionally or unintentionally, and great epic stories often follow how small events translated into gigantic changes in self, in others, or in their surroundings.

The thing that separates us from primates, the perception of time, is our ability to tell stories, by sharing what the cause and effect of certain actions are.

Why Does It Matter?

Our brain has been constructed through millions of years of

evolution, and even though two random people plucked from anywhere around the world will have thousands of differences between them based on race, religion, gender, sexual orientation, culture, age, how big their eyebrows are, and other factors, there will be one similarity amongst all of them.

Our brains are structured the same way.

It's this common structure that informs how we respond to stories.

Most people believe we will be interested in a story if it is a good story. I argue that a story is good if it conforms to how our brain structures information.

Examples: Pop Culture Movies

Over the course of this book, we've indirectly talked about *The Hero's Journey*. It's a story format derived from the research of Joseph Campbell on similarities in Eastern and Western religions, and has influenced *Star Wars*, *The Matrix*, the *Harry Potter* series of novels, and countless other books, films, and video games. At its simplest, it's about a hero leaving their ordinary world, crossing the threshold by entering a new, unfamiliar and challenging world, learning a valuable lesson (or attaining a valuable treasure), and returning to their previous world forever changed for the experience.

- In *Star Wars: A New Hope*, Luke Skywalker left his home planet of Tatooine, crossed into the new realm of exploring the galaxy, realized he had to save Princess Leia, escaped the clutches of the Galactic Empire, takes on a new identity as a pilot for the Rebellion, and returns to save the day and destroy the Death Star.

- In *The Matrix*, Mr. Anderson leaves his safe job to join Morpheus and the other rebels, chooses the red pill to venture into the new realm of the real world, realized he had to save Morpheus, escaped the clutches of Agent Smith, dies and resurrects to take on a new identity as Neo, and returns to master the world of the Matrix where he can now use his knowledge to fly.
- In *Harry Potter and the Sorcerer's Stone*, Harry left his home at 4 Privet Drive, crossed into the new realm of the Wizarding World, realized he had to prevent his parents' murderer Lord Voldemort from attaining the Sorcerer's Stone, passes the obstacles to get to the Stone, takes on a new identity as a wizard protected by his Mother's love, and returns to 4 Privet Drive a changed boy.

According to Campbell (and similar, earlier proto-structures like Otto Rank's and Lord Raglan's respective mythotypes) the hero of a story expands their known world (or known emotional state) by embarking on a great challenge, crossing the threshold into uncharted territory.

This is important because the "crossing the threshold" moment mimics child initiation rituals where a person is closing the door to an old way of life, a more naive way of life, and crossing the threshold into a new chapter; a metaphorical death and resurrection. Depending on the school of thought, this can also be a major part of Freudian psychology and psychoanalysis.

Our brains repeat this pattern over and over again as we symbolically pass through different chapters in life: new schools; new cities; new jobs; new relationships; etc.

If we follow this metaphor further, a mother goes through

great pain and sacrifice during childbirth, and out of it comes a new baby. Metaphorically, the mother's life as an individual ends, and a new life begins as a caretaker. In a literal sense, she is returning home with a new human, resurrected out of her own pain, suffering, and DNA that has forever changed her.

Now, as someone who grew up Catholic, I also see some similarities in how these thresholds overlap with the *Seven Sacraments* in Catholicism. They include the *Sacraments of Initiation* (Baptism, Confirmation, the Eucharist), the *Sacraments of Healing* (Penance, and the Anointing of the Sick), and the *Sacraments at the Service of Communion* (Marriage, and Holy Orders).

Think I'm reading too much into it? Well, Francis Ford Coppola used this same idea to juxtapose the sacraments with key moments in Michael Corleone's emotional journey in *The Godfather* trilogy.

I'm primarily talking about *The Godfather* (the first one, the good one) but this imagery is littered throughout the entire trilogy.

The Godfather opens with a wedding, which is designed to unite two people together in matrimony: this setting introduces Michael and his partner Kay, showing us the world Michael is trying to leave behind in his attempted courtship and future marriage with Kay. Later, Michael visits his father in the hospital, during Christmas, which one could argue is an Anointing of the Sick, showing us how Michael is compelled to return to this dark world in an effort to protect his family.

Later on, Michael has a wedding of his own with a woman who is not Kay, but that scene is quickly followed by the woman's violent death, highlighting Michael's commitment to the family and what it has done to him personally. At the end of the film, we see Michael's transformation into the Godfather via a series of violent executions of his enemies, while he is attending his nephew's baptism, which is meant to be a sacrament/celebration of life.

Coppola chooses to juxtapose these key story moments with the *Seven Sacraments* from the character's Catholic heritage to highlight key moments in Michael's transformation.

The hero's journey is resonant with us because it mirrors our own life, and by using this structure, we can dive into any topic, any conflict, and any world, because we've given an audience a path they can recognize and latch onto. It is a path that mimics their own lives, and a path that will make them care about the characters.

Road Map

The great thing about a road map is that you can hand it to anyone, and they can get directions to the same place you are going. They may take the scenic route. They may take the fastest route. They may take the route that drives by Shake Shack. Whatever route they take, they're going to get to the same place as you if you're both working off of the same road map, and that's how story structure works as well.

Components of Our Road Map

There are some key terms that make up a story's road map, starting with the smallest.

- **Beat** — In its broadest view, a scene is the smallest element of a story. Just as a heartbeat is crucial to life, story beats are vital to a narrative's vitality. They're the places where something important happens, where characters make decisions or face challenges, and where the plot takes unexpected twists.

• **Scene** — In film, it is a very technical term, because a new scene begins every time a character moves to a new room (or location), which is very important for logistical reasons (booking locations, moving the camera, etc.). In books, plays, and other media, it is usually considered a more fluid moment where characters exchange actions and dialogue. Every scene should have a beginning, a middle, and an end beat, and the best scenes serve multiple purposes in the story.

• **Act** — An act is like the chapters in a book; a major structural division. Different stories can have different numbers of acts demarcating the narrative's various phases: Plato had 3; Shakespeare had 5; Kubrick had 9; and don't even get me started on Christopher Nolan. Generally speaking, your act will structure how we are introduced to a world, how our hero interacts with that world, and how our hero's story ends.

• **Plot** — In the world of literature, theater, and film, the plot is the strategic sequence of events that weaves together a story. These actions unfold in a specific order based on external events, creating a sense of cause and effect that propels the story forward. I use the term "propel" because it often serves as an engine pushing our hero into new and uncharted waters, and there can even be multiple plots in a story. Princess Leia is trying to get the Death Star plans to the rebels. Cypher is betraying Neo and Morpheus. Harry discovers Voldemort is after the Sorcerer's Stone. It is the external goal in your story.

• **Character Arc** — A character arc is the internal transformative journey a character embarks on. Luke learns to trust his instinct through mastery of the Force. Neo learns to claim his identity and believe in himself. Harry realizes he needs his friends and loved ones to succeed.

One Last Caveat

I want to make clear, I am not advocating a strict interpretation of this story structure. Your first draft should pour out onto the page in its rawest form. This structure is meant as a reference for your second draft, when you take the raw clay you've placed on the page, and in an attempt to figure out what works and what doesn't, use this structure as a gap-filling device, to experiment and take your story in new places, with a new set of eyes you didn't have before.

Without further ado, I would like to lay out a consolidated structure, based on multiple formats I have researched.

1.   Open On Compelling Conflict/Action — Make a Promise in Tone and Plot

2.   Ordinary World — Make a Promise in Character Arc (What is the thing our character cannot have? Or doesn't know that they want?)

3.   The Call to Adventure — Establish Plot A

4.   Refusal of the Call
   • *At some point, characters A and B need to meet, and introduce the character conflict.*

5.   Supernatural Aid/Meeting with the Mentor

6.   Crossing the First Threshold

7.   Belly of the Whale — Establish Plot B

8.   End of Act 1

9. Beginning of Act 2

10. Road of Trials — Subplot
    • *Caught by the Death Star tractor beam*

11. Committing to the False Goal

12. Meeting with the Goddess — Subplot
    • *Find the Princess*

13. Woman as Temptress — Subplot

14. Midpoint twist, in which the stakes change dramatically/ Midpoint Twist, Reveal Secret Dealer.

15. Atonement With The Father — Subplot Payoff
    • *Death of Obi Wan*

16. Apotheosis — Possible twist that brings Plot B to the forefront

17. Go for the New Goal

18. The Ultimate Boon — Resolve Plot A

19. End of Act 2 — Possible twist that brings Plot B to the forefront

20. Beginning of Act 3

21. Refusal of the Return — Lowest point, hero believes absolute failure is unavoidable.
    • *Frodo refuses to give up the ring.*

22. The Magic Flight

23. Rescue from Without

24. The Crossing of the Return Threshold

25. Master of Two Worlds — Resolve Plot B

26. Freedom To Live

27. End of Act 3

Writing Exercise:

Write a list of scenes of your character doing something that other people would watch, and admire, or empathize with. Show your character taking action, and making choices that reveal to us something in ourselves.

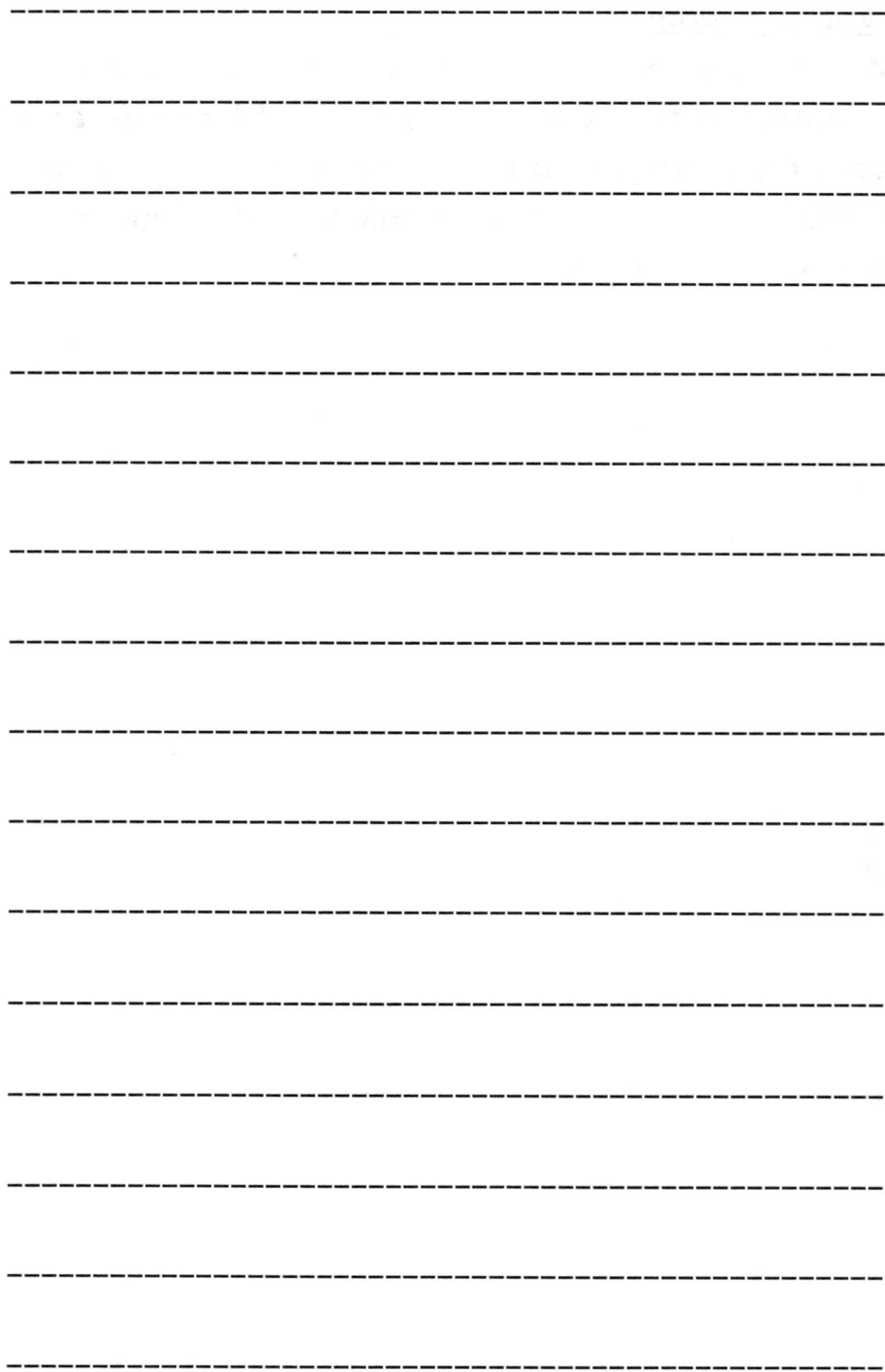

Open On Compelling Conflict/Action

Alright folks. Buckle up! Our first story beat is diving into the heart of the conflict, most often referred to as *The Cold Open.*

So, what is a cold open, you might ask? It's when a writer decides to throw you right into the thick of things at the start of a story. No fancy exposition, no long-winded explanations, just straight-up conflict. Sometimes this means an action sequence, but more often it means a dramatic conflict between your protagonist and their primary opposing forces. It's like jumping into a freezing cold pool without any warning. It's shocking, it's exhilarating, and it's a surefire way to grab your attention. Sometimes that's at the beginning of your story, sometimes it's a flash-forward to the middle.

The benefit of this is that when done right, you're exemplifying the old adage of showing your story, not telling it. We can see your hero's strengths and weaknesses. We can see your antagonist's overwhelming power and how they appear unstoppable.

Most often, people associate this with adventure and a fight scene, but it's not.

Remember, the opening of Indiana Jones? The giant boulder? That's exciting, but I would argue there are only two important parts in that opening sequence.

First, after Indiana Jones escapes the giant boulder, he's

confronted by his arch-nemesis, Belloq, who has used his deceitfulness to motivate the local villagers against Indiana Jones, stealing the idol from him. Yes Indiana Jones is cunning. Yes, he's brave. Yes, he's daring. However, it's not enough, because Belloq is even smarter, stronger, and more deceitful. He is willing to do anything to get what he wants.

This opening confrontation sets up everything we need to know about the characters, and creates a compelling villain for Jones to fight against.

The second important part is Indy screaming, "I HATE SNAKES, JOCK! I HATE 'EM!"

Now, you might be thinking, "But why do writers do this? Why not start with some exposition, set the scene, give me some context?"

Well, my skeptical friends, let me tell you: a cold open is the perfect way to set the tone for a story. It's like a litmus test for the audience. If you're hooked from the first few seconds, you'll stick around to see what happens next. If not, well, maybe this show isn't for you.

A cold open also allows writers to play with structure and pacing. By starting in the middle of the action, they can go back and forth in time, filling in the gaps as the story progresses. It's like a puzzle, and the audience gets to piece it together as they go along. Plus, it's just plain fun.

Who doesn't love a good mystery to unravel?

Here are some good tips and options when considering an opening sequence for your story.

- Make a Promise in Tone and Plot; clearly convey what the

story is going to be about.

- You can have your main character make a discovery. You can use this scene to reveal their strengths, but also show something they are missing.

- You could convey the crux of your story by omitting your protagonist. Choose to focus on your antagonistic forces and what they have been working on for our hero to discover later. Do we see someone toiling long into the night? This is a common nine-act structure plot point, where we reveal that the makings of this story have been set up long in advance, and it works well in David-and-Goliath or societal-transformation stories.

- The opening could only be tangentially related. The Indiana Jones opening sequence shows that the story is about adventure and golden archaeological artifacts, while still focusing on the primary and secondary characters.

- You could show the greater universe. In *Star Wars; A New Hope*, we see the Galactic Empire is evil, Princess Leia is fighting for democracy, and we need to get the plans to the people who will defeat them.

Writing Exercise

Write an opening scene for your story that sets up your character in the thick of it. It could be at the beginning of their story. It could be in the middle of their story. It could even be the first half of the final scene, but show us your character doing something they're good at, and taking action.

Meta-Messages

It's funny how you look at things in different contexts. When I was in high school, I loved independent films. Actually, I want to say non-studio films, because that's a broader and more accurate umbrella. This included weird little movies that would appear on the Independent Film Channel and HBO original movies, because they were so different and unique. They made you look at the world in a very different way, looking at little-known historical figures like Dorothy Dandridge, the Tuskegee Airmen, and original films like the America Ferrara film, *Real Women Have Curves*.

Amongst these, I loved the 1997 movie, *The Second Civil War*, which I thought was profound and prophetic, about how a second American civil war would break out over xenophobia and the issue of immigration. Then I re-watched it last year, having lived through the Trump Administration, and seeing the cruelty of life inflicted upon the many unsuspecting innocents, and I realized something else about the film.

Several of the characters are very silly, and don't act the way normal people do, BUT I was also able to see the way other characters were weighed down by their own failures and regrets. Each character had dealt with the cruelties of reality in a very distinct way, and the author was using that to convey their message.

I could understand that these histories were subtly conveyed in ways that only an adult could see, via something called a *meta-message*.

Meta-messages are a way of subtly using characters in your story, and their actions, to convey a message or lesson. This could be confused with subtext, which is what characters are saying without really saying it. So, here's a good shorthand:

- Subtext is the <u>character's</u> unspoken intentions
- Meta-Messages are the <u>storyteller's</u> unspoken intentions

Now, meta-messages relate to the structure of a story by looking at the character construction of the film.

I'm very grateful that I had the privilege of directing a feature film called *Unfriendly Fire*. In our film, we have characters who are part of the 'ultra-patriotic' right, who talk about the founding fathers, about America being a Christian nation, and who drape themselves in the American flag (literally, one character wears an American flag as a bandanna). However, these characters are also displayed as incompetent villains who use force and brutalism to exact their will.

On the other side, we have trans and queer resistance fighters who, at first, are very reluctant to support America, but as a conflict breaks out, they step up to defend America from the violent insurrectionists. In fact, one character, a non-binary person named Kit Brighton, says at the midpoint of the film, "We have to save America."

This juxtaposition makes a clear statement that the people who are represented by the flag-waving, ultra-patriotic are hypocrites, and the real Americans are the ones they target (LGBTQ+, trans, and BIPOC individuals).

While it is never said overtly that these villains (and the political factions they represent) are false-patriots out for themselves, it is implied through structuring the narrative around this dynamic.

Let's look at another example, the classic film, *Casablanca*. (Spoiler alerts for a cinematic classic that was released in 1942, and has inspired more romantic get-togethers than Barry White.)

In *Casablanca*, Rick is a former freedom fighter for democratic movements in Fascist Europe who has given up his noble causes to run a shady nightclub and casino in Casablanca. When he begins the film, he doesn't stick out his neck for anyone. Suddenly, his old flame, Ilsa, is in town with her husband, Victor Laszlo, a famed rebel with the Nazis on his tail. Ilsa knows Rick can help them get out of the country, and Laszlo offers him $100,000 francs for special passes to neutral Portugal (which would be well over $2 million in today's money). Rick eventually decides to deceive the parties, convincing them that he's taking the special passes to escape Casablanca with Ilsa as his lover, only to reveal that he is actually helping Laszlo and Ilsa escape together, where Laszlo can continue his work helping the resistance against the Nazis. In the final scene, Rick is saved, the head Nazi is killed, and Rick plans to leave to help freedom fighters across Africa and Europe to fight back against the Nazis.

There are several meta-messages made with the positioning of these characters in the narrative.

1. Nazis are bad and democracy is good.

2. It's never too late to do the right thing and get back into the fight.

3. Anybody can choose to do the right thing.

4. There are some things more important than money or love, and that includes the freedom of our fellow humans.

The concept of meta-messages was brought into the limelight by the English anthropologist, Gregory Bateson. He described it as communication about communication. Think of it as a message within a message, where you not only convey information but also give clues about how that information should be interpreted.

In the context of this chapbook of essays, meta-messages (or meta-communication) is the unspoken language that accompanies the words we utter, and it conveys the values of your story.

As a filmmaker, my bread and butter is meta-messages, because it serves as a visual shorthand to reveal character and power dynamics. It also is the answer to that age-old question of how to show and not tell (especially in a written form like a novel where, technically, all you're doing is telling). It also goes back to our original story with Tommy, where we discussed that the way in which the story was presented was just as important as the story itself.

But here's the kicker: meta-communication can be a tricky beast. It can be in sync with your spoken words, reinforcing your message, or it can be a sly trickster, contradicting everything you say.

For example, if you say, "Oh, that's just great!" with a derisive tone, that suggests the complete opposite, and then follow it with the listening character's reaction of disappointment, or even shame.

Because meta-communication can be very subjective, it can be seen one way by a teenager, and another way by a forty-year-old. It can be seen one way by someone who's British, and another way by someone who's Irish. It can be seen one way by someone who grew up in a diverse environment, and another way by someone who grew up in a very Caucasian and affluent suburb. That's the kind of paradox that meta-communication revels in.

In storytelling, this kind of communication works best with juxtaposition, where the combination of two images or actions speak volumes, compared to what either one of them would say on their own. It also has the added benefit of getting your audience intrigued, by having them decipher between the lines, rather than just saying, "Rick showed admiration for Victor Laszlo."

This is particularly important for people who are neurodivergent, as people who are dyslexic or autistic don't always pick up on sarcasm or other contextual clues in the same way as the majority of the population. Some might need these contextual clues to be spelled out for them. In fact, it's quite telling that Steven Spielberg, who has been applauded for his amazing visual prowess, creating stories and images that billions of people can see and understand, is in fact dyslexic and has talked openly about his dyslexia.

Another example of autistic creators is one of my favorite poets and authors, WB Yeats.

Prof. Michael Fitzgerald suggested in his book, *Autism and Creativity: Is there a Link between Autism in Men and Exceptional Ability?* (Bruner-Routledge, 2004) that the Irish author was autistic due to his documented reading and writing problems, and his poor school record (where he was bullied) but still had a great, vivid imagination while remaining socially aloof. As a result, Yeats' imagery and allusions in his poetry is powerful, and direct, leaving nothing open to interpretation. Essentially, because Yeats was (possibly) on the autism spectrum, his poetry was more direct, using less allusion and meta-messages than most authors, which allowed his work to be better popularized.

Yeats was also a fierce Irish nationalist at a time when Ireland was fighting for independence from England, often using his poems and stories to support the cause using indigenous Celtic imagery, believing the pen was mightier than the sword. If you read his most famous poem, "The Secret Rose", you can see his arguments for Irish independence with lines like, "And the proud dreaming king who flung the crown / And sorrow away, and calling bard and clown."

Yeats didn't rely on meta-messages, but often evoked imagery in his writings that inspired and incited Irish nationalist beliefs, such as Gaelic Faeries, the Faerie realm known as The Other World, and strong Christ-like representation which would resonate with the predominantly Catholic Irish population. This can be found in his short stories, "The Crucifixion of The Outcast" and "The Curse of The Fires and of The Shadows."

This evaluation of meta-messages requires storytellers to really evaluate how their characters' portrayal, and interactions with one another, affect their audience's sub-conscious interpretation of the world. Some might call this being "woke" (whatever the hell that means), and some might call this method overthinking it. However, in this controversial discussion, I say that you, as a storyteller, are putting yourself in a cultural leadership position whether you acknowledge it or not. So, as a storyteller, it becomes part of your job to overthink it, because you are leading an audience through your world view, and the behavior you feel people should emulate, like a Pied Piper of Hamelin.

Some might say that it's not the role of artists, filmmakers, and storytellers to engage in politics; and to those people I say, "Go fuck yourself" because:

A) you're dismissing someone's first amendment rights;

and B) artists have been talking about politics for centuries. Just ask Bob Dylan, Banksy, Ai Wei Wei, Frida Kahlo, and even Diego Velázquez from 15th century Spain.

Michelangelo's Sistine Chapel was an endorsement of the Catholic Church and the rule of Julius II over the Papal states. Shakespeare was, in many ways, the official propagandist of the British monarchy (have you ever wondered why Scotland was liberated from the cruelty of Macbeth with the help of the British army?). And don't even get me started on the Kevin Sorbo crime against cinema, *God's Not Dead*.

All stories are inherently political. Even stories that don't address politics, racism, or prejudice, are acting as a silent rubber stamp that the current political situation is A-OK.

So, ask yourself the question: "Do I, as a storyteller, believe the world is good exactly the way it is?"

If the answer is no, then we can start addressing how the world needs to change, through choices in our stories and our characters. I say "we" because we're in this together, and I'll help you wherever I can without telling you what to do. Because all I can do is show you the door, you're the one who has to walk through it.

Writing Exercises:

Write out something you saw in the last week that was the most unfair, or unjust thing. It could be as big as a war, or as small as a cop giving a bogus traffic ticket.

_____

_____

_____

_____

Now, write a list of characters who would embody that wrong. If you need help, go to the next page, but if you don't, skip to the next chapter (so as not to lead you into a specific direction).

_____

_____

_____

_____

_____

_____

Okay, if you're having trouble coming up with a list of characters, let's look at some possibilities.

If we use the example of a cop giving a bogus traffic ticket, let's ask who would be the people in that chain facilitating that bogus traffic ticket. There might be the cop who is giving the ticket because they don't like how the driver looks, but that's the easy one. Maybe the cop is just lazy and close to retirement so he's carrying out orders to give out bogus tickets by his supervisor. Maybe the supervisor is corrupt, and trying to bolster the revenue his department makes through tickets because he'll get a promotion. Maybe the police chief or sheriff is instructing cops to give out tickets to drive up revenue because he wants to run for mayor. Maybe the police chief is telling the cops to give out tickets in a certain part of town dominated by the poor, or a specific ethnic group that he hates. Maybe there's a city councilperson who wants the police to give out more tickets to bolster the city revenue, because he fought for lower taxes. Maybe the city councilperson was pressured into lowering taxes by the wealthy person who owns the factory, and doesn't care how the city makes up the lost revenue. Or maybe the sitting mayor of the city is prejudiced against a particular ethnic group, and wants the cops to give out tickets as part of a paranoid program to find (or make) criminals, similar to Mayor Bloomberg's Stop And Frisk policies in New York City.

With this method (on this specific example), you have a wide variety of characters, villains, and motivations to illustrate the power of corruption and systemic racism. Or, you could just give up and say it's a single villain like Red Skull trying to kill Captain America.

How Can You Use Meta-Messages in Setting to Convey Your Theme and Values

In a story, a setting is defined as a time and place, whether it's the deserts of the Middle East in 1936, present day America, or the virtual reality of a post-apocalyptic future.

As someone who grew up with Jewish heritage, the fear of persecution wasn't always physically present, but was often emotionally present, even in 1990's America. It didn't help that my Mother would often watch movies with me, and if there was a Holocaust reference, she would turn to me and say, "Just remember, if the Nazis came back today, they'd come for you too." And she wonders why I take medication for anxiety and high blood pressure.

Being multiracial and part middle-eastern didn't help either.

I like to joke with close friends that I'm just brown enough to get stopped every time at TSA. Literally, since 9/11, I've been getting suspicious looks for my "swarthy" appearance and have to arrive at the airport 4 hours before every flight as a precaution. Watching the security dogs and military commandos walk by with AK-47's was a reminder for all Americans that danger was afoot, but for myself, there was always a concern that the attack dogs and commandos would come after me. The looks of suspicion get to you after a while, where you feel if they can't trust you, then you can't trust anyone.

The threat of persecution has been especially present in the last several years, with increased graffiti of swastikas in 2017, the 2018 Tree of Life Synagogue shooting in Pittsburgh, the 2019 shootings at Chabad of Poway in California and Young Israel of Greater Miami, the rampant George Soros conspiracy theories in 2020, and so on, and so on. I had to argue with my future mother-in-law the reasons why there wasn't a Jewish banking conspiracy. She retorted with a straight face, "If there isn't really a Jewish banking conspiracy, why do so many people still believe that story?"

Even as recently as the time of this writing, in 2024, I would hear people (who didn't know I was Jewish) say, "I've given up on Bernie because he supports ISRAEL" with a tone on the word Israel that wasn't of remorse or even anger, but of visceral disgust, as if Israel's Jews were sub-human. In fact, it was very disappointing to find out how quickly my progressive friends would fall into the trap of Anti-Semitic stereotypes, with progressive organizers telling me to my face that Jews weren't a protected class because, "they own all the banks," a false stereotype that goes back to the Russian forged papers, *Protocols of the Elders of Zion*.

For this reason, it's always been easy for me to empathize with my African-American and Latinx friends who had their own concerns about the American police-state painting them as criminals, drug-dealers, rapists, and only occasionally "some good people." These were the stories specific to this time and place, which society told itself that caused them to interpret their fellow man as the enemy.

Counter-Storytelling

Thanks to important and valuable movements like *Critical Race Theory* (CRT), storytellers have been able to reexamine the connections between race, power, and societal structures.

Born in legal curriculum, it spread like wildfire, and sparked conflict and debate as it asked everyday citizens to reevaluate America's inherent biases, with inspiration from storytellers like Sojourner Truth, Frederick Douglass, W. E. B. Du Bois, and César Chávez; and yes, as we mentioned earlier, activist leaders are, by their very nature, storytellers. History is about Story.

The biggest takeaway from the movement has been *counter-storytelling*.

Now, let's not get too abstract about this. I want to talk about some concrete fundamentals and examples of counter-storytelling.

Example: Africa

Most American schoolchildren have grown up being taught that, historically, Africa had little technology, little scholarship, and made no significant contributions to world culture. I even remember my college economics professor at Chapman University say that the reason Africa never prospered in the world was because the rivers of Africa led inland to waterfalls, rather than smooth valleys as many of the European rivers did.

As an aside, while not the same professor, it's worth noting that Chapman University later provided us with Professor John Eastman, one of the indicted individuals who helped plan the

January 6th terrorist attack on the U.S. Capitol.

Stating that Africa never contributed to world culture is just flat out inaccurate and wrong. The fact is, Africa has had many great empires and scholars with advanced technology, whether it is the empire of lower Egypt with the great pyramids of Giza, or the lesser known Nubian pyramids of upper Egypt. There's also:

- The Mali Empire, whose scientists developed the first accurate astronomical calendar in West Africa in 300 BCE
- The rise of Islam in Africa which helped develop some of the most advanced mathematical scholars of the time around 700 CE
- The University of al-Qarawiyyin founded in 857 CE in Morocco
- Great city-states of East Africa, Kilwa, Great Zimbabwe, Benin, and Gondar, founded between 900 CE and 1200 CE
- The Zulu Kingdom in 19th century southern Africa
- The Kingdom of Kongo which had a commercial network that rivaled the Roman Empire, and lasted from 1390 CE to 1914 CE in southern Africa
- And the Ethiopian Empire, founded in east Africa in 1270 CE, which was seen as such an asset that Italy tried to invade it, twice

These facts are important parts of counter-storytelling that give us a richer and more accurate understanding of the world.

Why do we not hear about these?

Well, it's well-documented that Africa was plundered by their European neighbors for natural resources, including gold, diamonds, and human slaves.

How could they do that with a clean conscience?

The thing is, the human brain needs to (for lack of a better term) balance itself by making up logical fallacies in the process.

If Europe engaged in an ongoing campaign to plunder the kingdoms of Africa, destroying them for Europe's gain, Europeans needed to justify that behavior to themselves. So, Europeans invented a story that Africa was full of primitives who didn't really qualify as intelligent, or as people. This is where we got poems like "The White Man's Burden" by Rudyard Kipling, or the philosophy of the "noble Aryan Indo-European with blonde hair and blue eyes" that would go on to inspire Hitler.

The settings of these pieces of literature helped define the era of colonialism that lasted for hundreds of years.

However, you might be asking, why did we, as American schoolchildren continue to learn this into the 21st-first century?

Because we, as Americans, continued to adopt and rely on that philosophy for our own actions; first with slavery in the south, and then with voter suppression, as well as violent lynch mobs. Even northern cities had sundown towns into the 1970's, where African-Americans wouldn't be allowed after dark, creating a setting of a time and place that would distinguish the "good people" of the suburbs from those other people.

Setting is used as a way to define the in-group, and the "other". And so, in order to justify that terrible government oppression, we adopted a story that African-Americans were primitive Africans first, and Americans a distant second.

Writing Exercises:

Remember the list of characters you wrote in the previous essay? Now let's build the world in which they exist. Let's write about the world(s) they could make home. Come up with some attributes of the world that their lives would intersect with. Who has the authority and power? Who is the out-group? What does it look like? Is there special magic or technology that your characters depend on? If there isn't any magic, what do they depend on for their livelihood? Are there religions, political factions, or organized movements your characters believe in? What is your character's everyday life like?

Oh, and also, don't forget to be awesome.

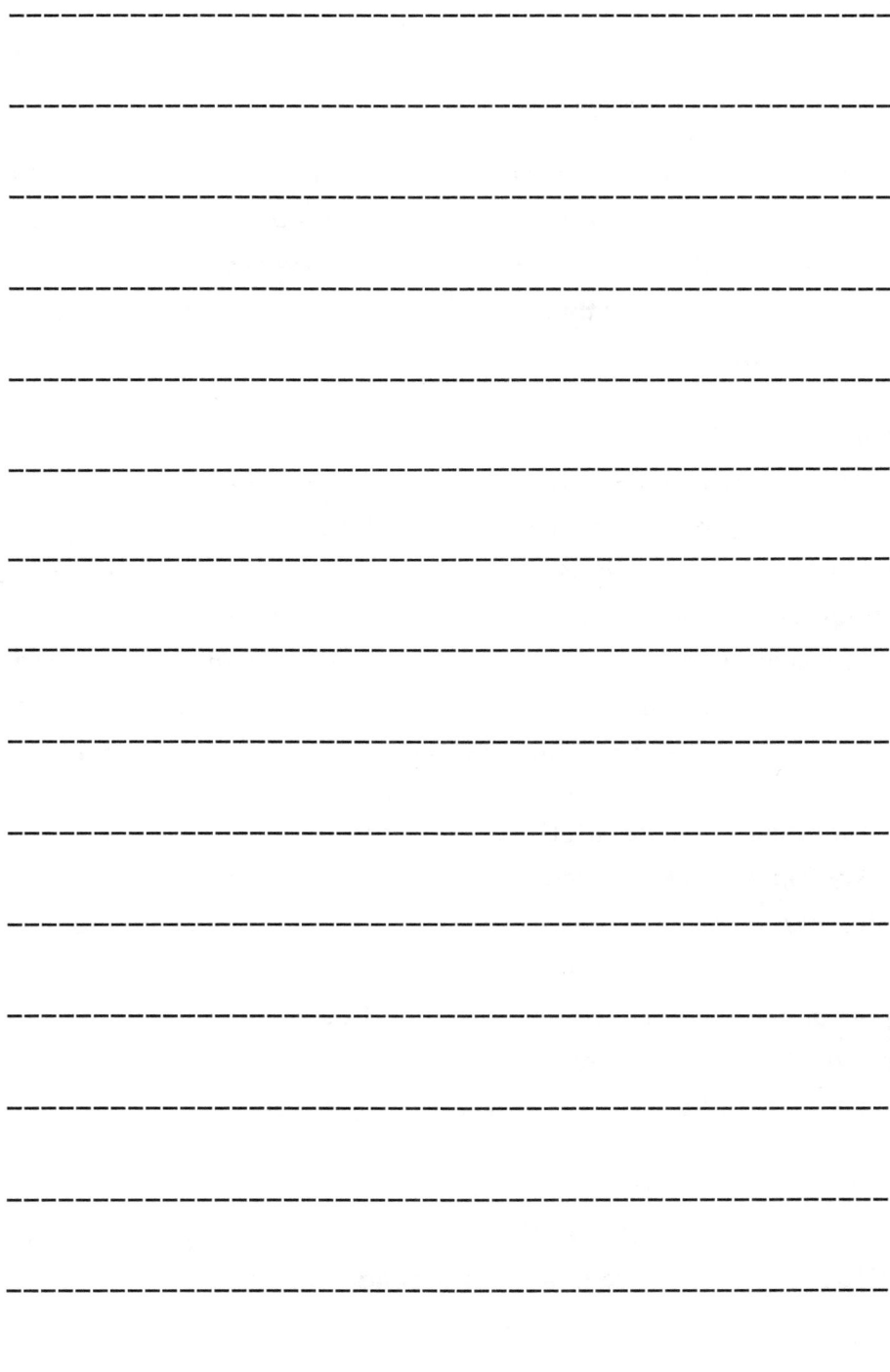

Why Does It Matter?

How we view others, and the settings in which we tell our stories, work to reinforce our own morality and gives us justification, and license, to do the things we do. That is why we need to reevaluate the storytelling tropes that we have seen and relied on for decades or even centuries.

This became brutally apparent to me as I matured as a storyteller. I found that some of my colleagues were telling stories that relied on the same tired tropes and in the same settings that had problematic implications. For example, setting fantasy stories in a magical version of medieval England that relied on stories of kings, queens, and royalty which ignored democratic governance. Another example is basing their stories in a troubled world, where a "chosen one" prophecy/archetype would save all the people.

Other examples included: hopeless romantic codependency's; token black/brown characters such as "the magical Negro"; dumb hippies/environmentalists as antagonists; etc. It was emotionally difficult seeing my friends repeat these tropes that had become part of our collective subconscious and also reinforcing negative stereotypes. These were stereotypes that I knew my friends did not believe in, but were still unintentionally perpetuating.

I realized that there was a better way to tell stories, and with a little guidance, these artists, filmmakers, and storytellers could retool their stories to change our collective narratives.

Example: *Unfriendly Fire*

I tried to implement these new ways of thinking about meta-messages in my own work, including in my own feature film, *Unfriendly Fire*, a comedy mockumentary about a second American Civil War set about 4 years in the future. I chose this time period because it was a direct commentary on our current political climate, and setting these kind of commentaries in the future (near or distant) has always been a tried and true method for satire.

While this may not seem related, I did try to carefully evaluate how my characters were portrayed, who was a good guy, who was a bad guy, and how they wound up in the position they were in, but I'm getting ahead of myself.

Unfriendly Fire was a feature film I made using this collaborative storytelling technique, where I assembled a rough outline, drafted characters, and then I brought in 8 talented, comedic actors to improvise the film's dialogue. I like this approach because, while I do consider myself a talented writer, as a straight, cis, white-passing male there are certain perspectives that I will never fully understand because society treats me in a very different way. For example, I will never be able to fully walk in the shoes of a Hispanic woman, mainly because Anna Valenzuela's shoes are way too small for me.

I will never know what it's like to be a queer African-American woman, or a trans-nonbinary person, but through this collaborative method, I can accurately represent those people on screen and in my story because I'm giving them agency, and letting them tell their own stories in their own words, within a setting and framework I constructed.

Some examples of this technique include actress Heather Meza discussing a real-life story about visiting a doctor when growing up in the South, where she was denied antibiotics because, even though she took a pregnancy test, her doctor claimed antibiotics can cause birth defects and a woman is always assumed to be carrying a child. Similarly, Anna Valenzuela talked about the real-life background of her grandmother who was a fierce environmental activist.

As a filmmaker, even though the story takes place in the South, I also took great pains to not paint all Southerners with a broad brush, or let my pro-North education create an unconscious bias towards this group.

I mentioned sundown towns in the North earlier, and I was brought up to believe that racism was mainly a Southern issue, but I was 39 when I found out that Darien and Greenwich, towns next door to where I grew up, were both anti-Black and anti-Jewish sundown towns, and some towns in Connecticut remained sundown towns until 1988.

In the film, *Unfriendly Fire*, the main villain, Adolf Miller (yes, I named him Adolf, and yes, the reason you're thinking is why), doesn't speak with a southern accent. In addition, we have one character who grows up very southern and home-schooled, and as a military-aged male, joins the insurrectionists, but I also went out of my way to cast another southern character who is a successful businessman and becomes a pro-Union spy.

I also lucked out in my casting of Steph LeHane as an organizer for AntiFa, the aforementioned nonbinary activist, Kit Brighton. Steph is a nonbinary actor who has a lot of experience in comedy, but I mainly cast them in this dramatic role because I knew that their charm from comedy would carry over to their performance and make them more likable.

By casting incredibly charming actors for the pro-Union, and pro-Antifa roles, I wound up creating a meta-message in the narrative that AntiFa are actually the good guys, which at the time of writing, is very contradictory to the mass-media narrative.

Now, this could come off like I'm bragging, which I am (look, making a feature film is fucking difficult, let me have this). However, let's look at another example of settings and meta-messages. Mel Gibson's *Passion of The Christ.*

Example: *Passion of The Christ* (Buckle Up!)

If you don't remember, *Passion of The Christ* was one of the most financially successful films of 2004, wedged in between *Spider Man 2* and *Harry Potter.* It was also incredibly divisive and controversial in its portrayal of certain characters who were Jewish, or not of traditional gender binaries. Now, I'm not going to focus on any of the well-documented anti-Semitic remarks from Mel Gibson, or his father, nor the fact that *The Passion Play* was historically an anti-Semitic play created in the fourteenth century. I want to solely focus on the meta-messages contained in the Mel Gibson film.

First, Jesus is portrayed by a charming and classically handsome actor, and he is seen as a leader of the 12 apostles who admire and follow him. Source-material aside, this sets a subconscious expectation in our brains that this is an attractive and noble person worth following. If Jesus were cast by a "traditionally unattractive" actor like Steve Buscemi, or Gilbert Gottfried, the audience would have had a very different reaction.

Satan then appears and tries to tempt Jesus, and Satan takes the form of an androgynous woman. I hope it's obvious that when you depict the literal embodiment of evil as an androgynous woman, you're setting up certain precepts in your audience's mind. Later in the film, we also have Herod Antipas, Jewish ruler of the Galilee, a client state of the Roman Empire, and Herod is depicted as an effeminate stereotype, clearly coded as a gay villain.

Then we get to the Jewish rabbis/leaders, and Mel Gibson has chosen to portray the Jewish temple in which they meet as a dark and shadowy place, often lit by torches. This meta-message conveys that these men are not to be trusted. He also cast the rabbis with actors who are fat, old, and traditionally ugly. While traditional beauty standards have been worth discarding for some time, filmmakers know that in a visual medium, attractive people are inherently seen as good, and unattractive people are inherently seen as flawed or bad. However, Mel Gibson also chose to expand the role of the rabbis in his film. Whereas they only appear briefly in the gospels, they appear VERY frequently in many locations in the film (not in every scene, but definitely in every sequence).

This meta-message is another indication of relevance to the overall story. The more locations someone appears, the more important they are. Similarly in photography and painting, the larger a person or object is in the frame/canvas, the more important they are.

The Jewish leaders are also constantly encouraging Pontius Pilate to do more harm to Jesus in the most violent ways imaginable. By contrast, Pontius Pilate is cast as a young and classically attractive man, as opposed to the old and ugly rabbis. The film actually has several scenes that seem to exonerate Pontius Pilate, and by extension, the Roman Empire that ruled over Israel with an iron fist. At the end of the film, it is not the Roman barracks or Pontius' headquarters that are punished, but the Jewish temple that is struck with an Earthquake, cracking the mighty stone floors and pillars (and they say subtlety is dead).

The film also goes out of its way to portray the Jewish citizens of Galilee as cruel and uncaring. They demand that Jesus be crucified while Barabbas (a thief and murderer who is cast with overt and exaggerated stereotypical Jewish features) is released. They raucously chant and taunt Jesus in his march to the crucifixion, embodying the idea that the Jews are cruel Christ Killers who do not deserve sympathy.

The film also portrays Judas, a Jewish man, as clawing and money grubbing while on the floor as the rabbis throw his payment in silver coins at him, spilling out for Judas to supplicate for.

While I understand this is an interpretation of the source material, look at how a similar film covered this same action.

In *Jesus Christ Superstar*, Judas initially rejects the "blood money" payment in silver, until he's told he could give the money to charity, at which point he starts to reconsider. Even though the rabbis drop the payment on the ground, *Jesus Christ Superstar* does not show Judas picking up the coins. In addition, the rabbi's temple in *Jesus Christ Superstar* is portrayed as bright, open-air, and lit by daylight.

Passion of The Christ conveys a meta-message that our villain, Judas the Jew, is greedy and money hungry. *Jesus Christ Superstar* conveys a meta-message that Judas is giving into temptation, doing a bad thing for good reasons.

Then we get into the violence, and yes, 33 CE was a time filled with cruelty and violence. However, *Passion of The Christ* is filled with visceral, brutal violence towards Jesus, beyond the scope of what is portrayed in the gospels. There's an unbearably long torture scene portraying Jesus' flogging, including one shot where a chained flogger rips flesh off his abdomen.

Now, here's the thing about violence, human beings tend to sympathize with other human beings if they are suffering. It's a hard-wired mechanism in our brain that really only turns off if we dehumanize those who are suffering by saying, "They're a criminal, they're Christ-killers, they're from a continent full of primitives who didn't really qualify as intelligent, or as people." So, when the audience sees Jesus suffering, we sympathize with him and develop a hatred of the people committing the suffering. With the increased presence of the rabbis, and the direct violence committed by the rabbis in striking and spitting on Jesus, it therefore sends a meta-message that the noble person worth following is being tortured by the cruel Jews.

Conclusion

There are several ways you can use your choice of setting, location, time, and other environmental factors to convey your theme (and I didn't even get into fantasy world-building, which could have its own book).

Above are several examples, but following are several bullet points that will help you decipher what different locations and time periods mean in the context of your story.

- Create settings that intersect with characters and their conflicts. What your character cares about is what your readers will focus on. What will be a source of passion for the main character, and what will the audience find awesome?

- The more realistic you want the story to feel, the more you should set it in a real place and time (the past, or the present).
- If you are criticizing a society or societal attribute, set it in the future, in a time and place where the thing you're criticizing has taken over and turned our world into a dystopia, so your hero can rebel against it.
- If you want your audience to feel a sense of wonder and whimsy, you can use magic with no discernible rules (also referred to as a *soft magic system*).
- If you want your hero to seem small at the beginning of your story, place them in a very large world, of epic statues, kingdoms, buildings, mountain ranges, etc. The bigger the obstacles they overcome, the bigger their transformation will be.
- If you want your hero to seem big at the beginning of a story, place them in a very small world, similar to *Gulliver's Travels*.
- If you want your character to seem an unlikely leader at the beginning of your story, place them in a royal court, in the lap of luxury, where they will have to sacrifice their comfort in order to help their people.

Remember the list of characters you wrote in the previous essay? Now we're going to take two of those characters who are the opposite, because good conflict comes from opposites. Pick two characters, and write a scene in which each character is making a choice to pursue something, and preferably something tangible. They could be the same thing. They could be different things. They could know about what each one is pursuing, or not find out until halfway, or the end of the scene.

How do your characters meet? Where do they meet? How do they interact? Does something they learned change how they interact with each other?

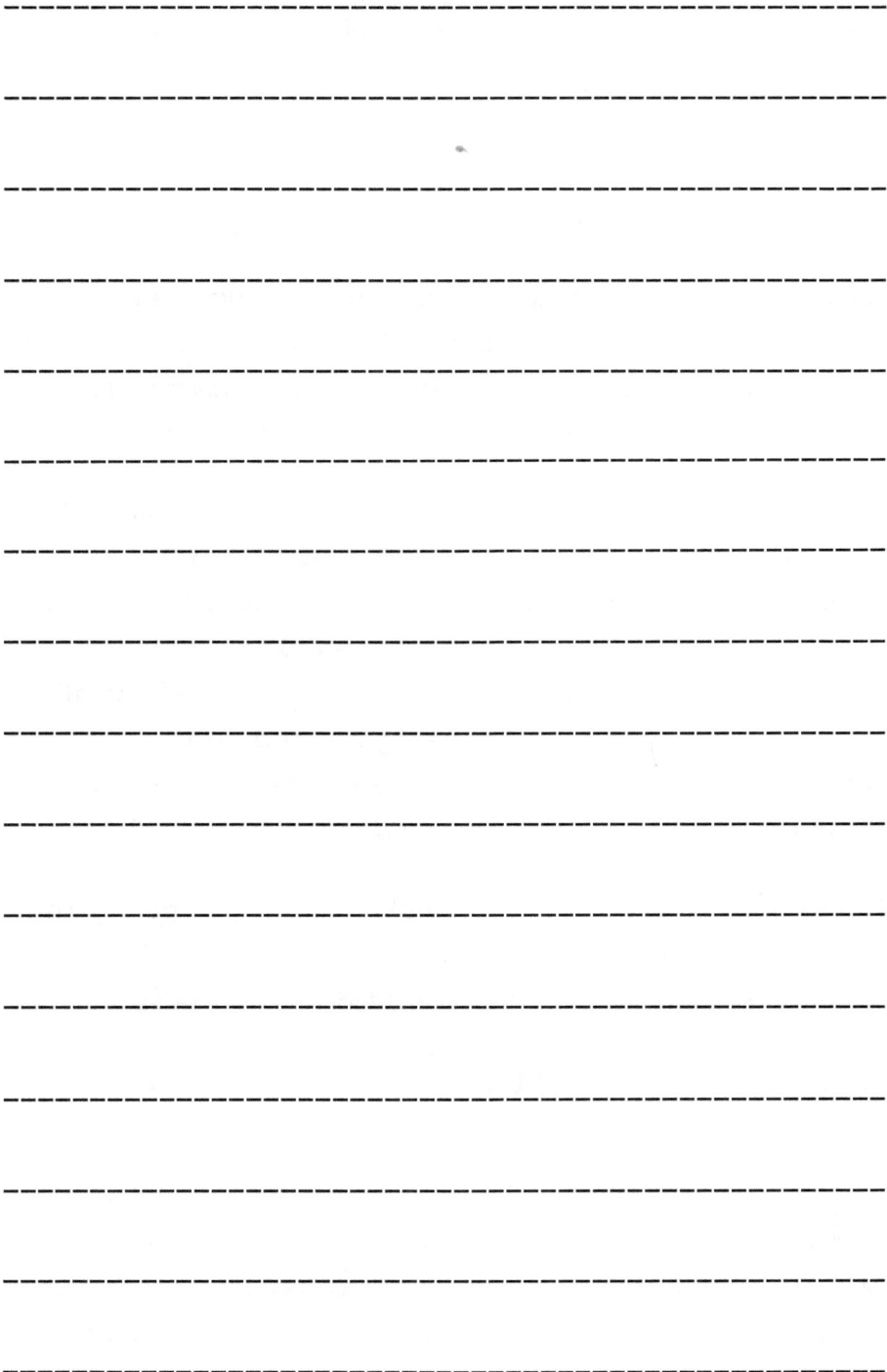

Trans-Media Storytelling:
Exploring Your World Through Multiple Eyes

In 2021, I had just broken up with my fiancé, and was dealing with a very serious depression. As an outlet, I would apply to almost any paid creative opportunity online (as long as they didn't ask for my social security number—I was depressed, not stupid).

I applied to essay positions, art shows, all sorts of things. One such opportunity was a company called Tongal, who was building out their YouTube content. I dusted off an old idea of mine, a hard hitting documentary about my experience in reality television, called, *Behind the Reality Curtain*, dealing with how I saw contestants being abused and crew being underpaid. I retooled it to be a mockumentary about reality TV, which used satire and improv comedy to make fun of it.

To be honest, I was so certain that I wouldn't get the gig, that I submitted a treatment that was just a blank page (because I said in the pitch I was going to use all improv comedians).

About a month later, I got the job.

¯_(ツ)_/¯

I used this paid opportunity to make a short film version of my larger project, which could then be used as a Proof of Concept. Because it was tied to larger ideas and themes, it wound up being a hit. The short film was in the top 10% most watched videos on their channel. I used this process again and again to explore characters and ideas that I had larger projects for, directing a total of 5 projects for Tongal at time of writing. This method is referred to as *Trans-Media*.

Trans-Media storytelling (also referred to as trans-media narrative or multi-platform storytelling), is a technique that allows a single story to be experienced across multiple platforms and formats through the eyes of multiple characters. This can be a unique and interesting twist on communal storytelling, by creating a road map to your story world and allowing other storytellers to play in your fictional sandbox.

What Does It Look Like?

You may be most familiar with this from big enterprises like the *Marvel Cinematic Universe*, where the same characters exist along the same narrative, but viewed from different perspectives in television, feature films, short films, and comic books. However, it is equally possible for a shared universe to exist in other formats, including books, podcasts, web series, and even sound art.

Thanks to the wonders of current digital technologies, a story does not have to be limited to one format, allowing big story worlds to be depicted at different scales through different formats.

In other words, if you want to make a big Marvel-style movie, and don't have $300 million to burn (which I assume most of you don't, and if you do, give me a call), you can still find a format that is more conducive to your budget, that takes place in the same story world, and with different characters.

If you want to tell big, ambitious stories, you can use trans-media storytelling to do it based on the means you have available.

What makes this technique truly exceptional is that each piece of the overall chronicle is not only connected with the others (either overtly or subtly) but also has the same visual look. This allows for different storytellers to helm each piece, as long as they follow the road map set out by the major creators.

From my own experience, the key to this collaborative storytelling is to create a road map that has important guidelines, but allows the guest creatives to build out their own unique depictions.

For example, if you're making an interplanetary sci-fi story, the road map says there's a planet called Gold-Fiend that is 90% ocean, where the local civilization worships water-deities, but has gold and other precious metals at the bottom of the oceans. However, the guest creator can identify what their form of government is, which leads to the question of, is there a protagonist who needs to root out or overturn corruption? What is daily life like? What do the cities look like? What do the people do for fun? What are the key values that those people believe in? Etcetera.

From a production standpoint, it is often used in marketing strategies by creating additional media projects that capture the attention of the audience through a variety of techniques, which permeate their daily lives; essentially creating unique events and scenarios to go where viewers will find it (theaters, TV, web, TikTok, or podcasts), rather than blasting out your message through traditional advertising to make them come to you.

In other words, trans-media storytelling is an approach that transcends the traditional boundaries of storytelling, whose goal is to immerse and capture an audience in a narrative universe that extends far beyond a single show or book. It's the perfect way to keep an audience engaged and excited about learning more about a story and its characters, through the lenses of different artists.

One great historical example of this is the 1605 book *Don Quixote*. This much-beloved tale of a delusional, middle-aged man who fancies himself a knight actually had early versions of fan fiction written using the characters. This was a problem in the eyes of Miguel de Cervantes, so much so that in 1614, an author (or group of authors) writing under the name Alonso Fernández de Avellaneda published an unauthorized sequel entitled, *Second Book of the Ingenious Knight Don Quixote of La Mancha*.

Cervantes became so enraged that he published a canonical second book the following year, where Don Quixote learns of Avellaneda's book and is outraged by the way it portrays him. From then on, the Avellaneda publication is ruthlessly mocked over the course of that book.

For example, Don Quixote avoids going to a jousting tournament because such an event took place in the Avellaneda edition and, at another point, Don Quixote even meets a character from Avellaneda's work, Don Alvaro Tarfe, and gets him to sign an affidavit that the two have never met before.

While this humorous take down was richly enjoyed by those of 17th century Spain, Cervantes had inadvertently canonized Avellaneda's book into the *Don Quixote* story world, making it a great example of trans-media storytelling.

The Science

One of the reasons this method of storytelling is so effective is that the human brain receives dopamine chemicals when we recognize things. What is dopamine? Well, it's a natural chemical in your brain and a type of neurotransmitter that can improve blood flow. However, what it does in the body is, it makes you feel good and gives you a sense of pleasure. It also gives you the motivation to do something when you're feeling pleasure.

Dopamine has been associated with everything, including chocolate, cocaine, watching TV, BDSM, religious gatherings, and getting extra likes on Facebook posts.

In short, our brain feels pleasure when we are rewarded, OR when we recognize something we've previously seen or experienced.

You might be asking yourself, "Self, where's the actual proof?"

Well, researchers at the Center for Brain Health and colleagues in Sweden have discovered a link between the brain's dopamine system and the ability to recognize faces.

Led by Dr. Bart Rypma, the study found that the level of dopamine in the fusiform gyrus predicts facial recognition ability. This is the first time a connection has been made between dopamine and facial recognition.

Consequently, anytime someone recognizes a character, a location, or even an object from another story, and makes the connection in their brain, a small amount of pleasure is released.

Has there ever been a time when you were watching a movie,

you recognized a location in that movie you had visited, and then became excited and happy that you recognized it?

That biological function lends itself to trans-media storytelling, because people keep recognizing characters, locations, and objects from other stories. This also leads us to the *Easter Egg*, and no, I'm not talking about the chocolate.

An *Easter Egg* is a hidden feature, message, or image tucked away within a narrative, waiting to be discovered by the keen-eyed observer. It originally came from the 1979 video game "Adventure" for the Atari 2600. The game's creator, Warren Robinett, secretly inserted his name into the game at a time when developers were not credited (similar to Al Hirschfeld hiding his signature in his character drawings). Players who found a hidden room discovered the message, thereby unearthing one of the first-known Easter Eggs in the digital world. They add an extra layer of depth to the narrative, rewarding those who are familiar with the mythology.

Intertextual Connections can also create connections between different myths or cultural stories via Easter Eggs. They serve as a nod to the interconnected nature of mythologies, showing that these stories often share themes, symbols, or characters, and can be an exciting experience for an eager audience. It creates a sense of participation and discovery, drawing readers or viewers deeper into the story.

How You Can Use It

This strategy can especially help independent filmmakers, because even if you have a story and a character with a huge scope, you can still find an audience for your work by focusing on an adjacent story that's a prequel, sequel, or running in parallel to the main story you want to tell. This allows you to find an example of a story in that world that adheres closer to your (probably lower) budget and technical capabilities. Here are a few examples of projects I've pitched or been involved in that utilized this strategy.

The TNT show, *Snowpiercer*, was launching a marketing campaign to empower filmmakers of color, specifically asking them to direct short films related to the show. I pitched a concept called "Chess" focusing on a series of flashbacks looking at the main character, Andre, as he learns from his mentor, Old Ivan, and flashbacks to Old Ivan's life, during a game of chess that they play.

This prequel would have taken place years before the main show began, but would have attracted a new audience by dealing with heady intellectual topics, like leadership, hope, and the nature of freedom. Also, because the amount of filming needed for the main cast would have been minimal, it could be shot on a lower budget, focusing on Old Ivan in his younger days, when he could have been played by a different (cheaper) actor. TNT liked it so much that they purchased it from me, and hired two other filmmakers as well, who told their unique stories independently from one another, but in the same world.

Another example was one year when I went to San Diego Comic Con with the express intent of seeking out high-concept projects that could be made for independent micro-budget prices. The theory was we could make a feature film for a low enough budget as a proof of concept, and then secure higher funding to either embellish it with additional high-production scenes, or turn the sequel into the big, wide-release hit.

I almost bought the film adaptation rights for one comic book about a woman who rode around in a tank in a post-apocalyptic wasteland (no, it wasn't *Tank Girl*). I asked the author if there was a version of the story that could be made entirely in a single room, and he responded, "Yes, because she talks over radio with her partner in an orbiting satellite throughout the comic, so we could do a suspense story from his perspective."

That is a perfect example of trans-media.

The simple fact is, while many of us would love to make a huge movie, TV show, or video game, making something of epic scope requires hundreds of people over a prolonged period of time, and people have a nasty habit of wanting money for superfluous things like rent and food.

It is much easier and cheaper to take your epic story and write out a book, or produce an audio podcast, or a vlog-style web series, that tells a similar story that is not reliant on the visual crafts.

Franchise guru, Jeff Gomez, is behind *Pirates of the Caribbean*, *Tron Legacy*, and other major cinematic worlds, and has also advocated that new story worlds should be put out as audio first (podcasts, audio books, etc.), to build a cult following of loyal fans. If you choose to do this, then the medium is going to affect the writing of the initial chronicle that exposes us to that world: an audio podcast would be focused more on dialogue, whereas graphic novels focus more on the visual aspect and strange worlds.

Sometimes, audiences feel as though trans-media story lines leave gaps in plot lines or character development. In such instances, the audience can create their own extensions of trans-media storytelling with fan fiction, or even fan-made movies.

Another important aspect are hierarchies or skill levels that can be mastered, not by the artist, but by the audience. People want to gain experience, grow, and ultimately become masters in the world they explore. Consider how this would work for *Pirates of the Caribbean*: if you could experience the world from the perspective of different roles, say from cabin boy to crew member, first mate and ultimately captain, that would give you both a richer experience and something to strive for.

Through this interactive format, or even a more passive method of absorbing and memorizing trivia, a storyteller emboldens the audience to become messengers and continue to tell the story of the world on their own.

Consider your story and ask yourself if any of the characters are compelling or interesting enough to have a backstory that an audience would want to watch transform into the character we find in your main narrative. This can be used for prequels to your main epic story.

Next, take a look at the list below. It's a list of possible media formats, with the more expensive ones being accentuated (with the admitted caveat that expensive is subjective). Ask yourself if any of your characters could shine in the below formats?

Literature
(detailed world building)

- Hidden Journal
- Collection of Short Stories (Anthology)
- Literary Sequel (a bridge between a first movie and a

second movie)
- Fan Fiction
- Tabletop Role Playing Adventure (sometimes referred to as a *Module*)
- **Serialized Comic Book**
- **Large Graphic Novel**
- Novelization of Movie
- **Interactive eBook**
- Online Blog (Character, 1st Person)

Web
(marketing, possibly in tandem or lead up to release)

- Vlog (example: *Lizzie Bennet Diaries*)
- Mock-Reality
- Podcast
- Standard Single-Camera Format
- **Standalone Short Film** (testing ground for a supporting character's future project, a lá *Agent Coulson* or *Agent Carter*)

Video Game
(with the many free game engines out there, many video game formats are becoming more and more affordable to create)

- Vintage Arcade Game
- Phone App
- **Occulus Rift Experience/Game**
- Shooter (First Person or Third Person)
- **Massive Multiplayer Online Role Playing Games**
- **Strategy**
- **Musical** (example: *Rock Band*)
- **Simulation** (example: *Sim City, The Sims, Civilization*, etc.)

- Puzzle (example: *Tetris*)
- Platform (example: *Frogger*, *Portal*)
- *Fighting*
- *Racing*
- *Sports*
- Survival/Horror (example: *Silent Hill*, *Siren*, *Resident Evil*, *Clock Tower*, and *Parasite Eve*)

Live Performance

- Flashmob
- One Man Show
- Two Man Show
- *Immersive Experience*
    - *Theme Park Ride*
    - *Haunted Hayride*
    - *Overnight Experience*
- Traditional Stage play
- *Musical* (think "quirky, spectacle-driven," like *Repo*, or *Rocky Horror Picture Show*)
- *Opera*
- *Concert*

Feature Film

- *Micro-budget Feature* (scrappy, gritty, trying to change the world)
- *Low Budget Independent Feature* (scrappy, gritty, still trying to change the world)
- *Big Studio Feature* (a bigger-than-life experience, like *Lord of the Rings*)
- *Anime Feature* (good for surrealism, magical realism, etc.)

TV

- ***Live Action Episodic TV Show*** (Single Camera)
- ***Live Action 2-Hour Special*** (a *Backdoor* Pilot)
- ***Animation Series*** (Which format works best for your story?)
    - *Cell vs. CGI*
    - *Stop Motion*
    - *Live Action and Animation Mixed*
- ***Faux Reality Show***
- ***Serial*** (think soap opera or telenovela, like *Dark Shadows* or *Lost*)
- ***Multi Camera TV Show***

In his book, *You're Gonna Need a Bigger Story*, Houston Howard humorously describes trans-media storytelling as the art of extending a story across multiple mediums and multiple platforms in a way that creates a better business model for creators and a better experience for the audience. Because if there's one thing we know, it's that every story is better with a little bit of merchandising thrown in.

Trans-media researchers, like Professor Henry Jenkins of the University of Southern California, also highlights the ability of trans-media to attract a wider audience, using DC Comics' coloring books as an example of their strategy to appeal to younger audience members.

Scandal

If you're interested in more about trans-media storytelling theory, you can read works by the brilliant Henry Jenkins. As new media and platforms continue to emerge, the definition and methodologies of trans-media will continue to evolve and the term can be applied to seemingly similar but distinct phenomena.

It is important to distinguish trans-media storytelling from traditional, cross-platform media franchises or media mixes. If you are telling the same story but in different formats like a novelization of the film *Home Alone 2* (yes that's a real example, don't @ me), then that is classified as cross-platform storytelling, because it is the same story. However, if you're telling different stories in the same story-world, but with different characters and different character arcs, then that is trans-media storytelling.

There is even some debate in the storytelling community about what does and doesn't count as trans-media. Some believe that sequels and prequels do not qualify as trans-media, because they are a continuation of the characters and format, rather than entirely new expansions with different characters.

While we are most familiar with this approach from big blockbuster behemoths, this strategy of crossover characters and synchronized events between many stories has existed as long as history itself. In an interview with Professor Henry Jenkins and Matthew Freeman, Jenkins writes:

> There's no denying that the notion of stories that span multiple platforms predates the dawn of the twentieth century. Derek Johnson and Roberta Pearson, in particular, point to the mythological narratives of Ancient Greece and to the cross-platform narrative architecture surrounding the figure of Jesus Christ as possible (almost prehistorical) forms of trans-media storytelling. Mark J. P. Wolf also points to things like Homer's *Odyssey* as a story-

world that exists trans-medially and trans-historically.

The heart of trans-media storytelling lies in the creation of complex worlds that can sustain multiple characters and plot lines over extended periods of time. Each of these plot lines can be elaborated on by a different storyteller, and in a different format, adding rich depth to the world being created.

Writing Exercise:

Does your story have supporting characters, or unique locations? Choose 5 of the non-italicized story mediums (i.e. the cheaper ones) that would be good explorations of your supporting characters, or unique locations. Or, you can also choose one of the mediums as a prequel story for your main character.

Develop a Franchise Mythology

As a kid, I loved classical mythology. Before Wikipedia existed, I would go on deep dives at my local library, researching ancient lore of Greece, Egypt, and Roman gods. Eventually, I would dive into the exciting and often overlooked mythologies of Mesopotamia, India, and sub-Saharan Africa, trying to weave those stories into my own. For example, I wrote a screenplay called *El Diablo*, where a group of Hispanic med-students were invited to the home of a wealthy Caucasian benefactor to receive med-school scholarships. However, it turned out she was a witch, and invited them there to absorb their power and intellect.

On the surface, it's a standard haunted house horror movie, but in writing it, I used the archetype of *Hansel and Gretel* as the main inspiration. I also built scenes and sequences around Eastern European Jewish folklore (which I am descended from) and tales of rebirth and reincarnation from the Arab world. These kind of allusions help give a second layer of depth to the overall story, which makes the world feel larger and connected to real world mythology.

Continuing on the idea of trans-media storytelling, a franchise mythology is a comprehensive document talking about your story world. It includes the do's and don'ts of your world, and much of the backstory about it, and how it relates to your world's central theme. This harkens back to our previous chapters where we discussed reinforcing theme through various methods, and looking at archetypal characters throughout history. Some of the questions you can ask yourself to build your franchise mythology include:

- Who are the main characters of your world, and how do they relate to the theme?
- What are the most important locations of your world, and how can they expand on the initial concept?
- What is the era and style of your world, and how does it accentuate the message of your world?

Let's take an example from the world of television. For each new television series, the head creative, referred to as a *Show Runner*, writes a guiding document for the show with various important segments to influence its execution: Who are the characters?; What is the setting?; What is the characters backstory?; What are some examples of episode stories/springboards?; etc. This helps to guide multiple individuals as they work collaboratively to help write, direct, edit, and design the show. This document is called a *Show Bible*.

For a franchise, a similar document could be created, but because the concept is still fairly new in the creative landscape, the exact content and format is much more fluid. So, while I'm outlining this process, please note that you don't need to do it if it feels like a burden. In addition, what the franchise mythology document looks like for each story-world could be drastically different, ranging from a simple list of bullet points, to a 20 page detailed document with image samples and character quotes. Some people have even created a 300 page franchise bible for projects, and let me just say, please, dear God, don't do that unless you're being paid to create it.

There are a few key differences between a *Show Bible* and a *Franchise Mythology*, in that, with TV shows there's very little incentive to look beyond one season or even one episode. There are very different pay structures that define what a story arc will look like. However, franchises and story-worlds establish minimal rule sets (that which you cannot do), and also maximum rule sets (that which you must do). Would Luke Skywalker choose to take a life? No. Would Luke Skywalker always choose the morally right thing, even if it's difficult and dangerous? Yes.

Practical Tip: One great thing to remember about these franchise mythology documents is that you can copy and paste lengthy stories from public domain mythology, and add it to your own mythology document. Just make sure you include a smart-table of contents that auto updates with header text added.

According to Jeff Gomez, this element is referred to as a distant mountain, a term based on Tolkien's work: when Gandalf is leading the Fellowship through Middle Earth, he can point to some mountains in the distance and tell the group in detail about the backstory related to those mountains. This removes the feeling of walking through a "cardboard set" to get to the next plot point. Instead, we experience the richness of the world, it peaks our curiosity and makes it feel more real. It also plants seeds that may or may not grow into new plot points or future branches of the franchise.

Keep in mind, not every backstory needs to be created at the moment you write a passing reference on the page, but it helps to have some allusions to a greater world.

Gomez reminisces about a line from the original *Star Wars* movie where Obi Wan explains he fought in the Clone Wars as a Jedi

Knight with Luke's father. For twenty years, people wondered about those Clone Wars, and ultimately it gave George Lucas the opportunity to expand on his original universe in the prequel trilogy.

Other examples of distant mountains are Dorothy's ruby slippers from *The Wizard of Oz*, the bumps on the foreheads of Klingons in *Star Trek,* and the hat and whip of Indiana Jones.

Keep in mind, all of this is in service of working collaboratively. If one person had to create every *Star Wars* book, TV show, movie, and video game, then nothing would ever get done, and any finished work would be pretty stale, since it is just coming from one person. However, by welcoming in other people and fresh perspectives to our creative universe, we make our own works rich and deep with detail. By giving these other artists and participants a guiding bible, it points them in the direction of North, while allowing them to go East and West, but never South.

While the structure is very fluid, some of the key components of a franchise mythology bible can include:

- *Franchise Logline*: It defines the attributes of the intellectual property, both in terms of status quo and thematic underpinnings, so we understand what the property is. A franchise logline should be one or two sentences that describe the entirety of the story-world.
- *Archetypes, Messages, and Themes*: This is the brand essence chapter, the tone that we spoke about earlier. Some may see this as too academic, but it is very important to have. Each character should have a fact sheet on their archetypes. Jack Sparrow, for example, focuses on the character as possessing the traits of the trickster, always struggling to balance good and evil.

- *Overview of the Universe*: A summary of the world and its historic context, a profile of your lead hero(es) that summarize the life of the character from their perspective. Don't be afraid to provide statistics and/or core data on the character, skill sets, proficiencies, etc.
- *Supporting Cast, Villains, and a Bestiary*: Creatures, monsters and other entities that inhabit your world. Then, provide profiles of locations featured in the franchise and a survey of beyond (a hint at some distant mountains). One excellent example of this is *TalDorei Campaign Setting*, written by Matt Mercer and discusses characters and creatures of his fictional world.
- *An Extensive Section on the Magic and/or Super-Science of Your World*: The fantastical aspects of the world are explored and explained with parameters. What are the rules of how the magic system works? What cannot be done? What must be done? You have to think about what the principles that govern the impossible in your story-world are, because the moment you say "well, it's just magic," your audience starts losing interest, especially a younger audience. The job of kids is to ask questions of the narrative. If you fail to answer these questions beyond "it just is," you create a disconnect and fail to bring a sense of logic to the fantastic.
- *Chronology*: The thing that distinguishes a movie from a story-world is that multiple installments can occur over an extended timeline. A timeline of major events in the story world and areas for further exploration is a good resource to have, even if it is a high-level overview. This can be used for different, future endeavors, but also just to give more authenticity to the story. Some get fleshed out and can become referenced in ancillary IP. You can derive narrative chase elements from this: story hooks or cliffhangers.

If you are assembling your franchise mythology, here are some questions to ask yourself, and some sections you could contain:

- Who are the important characters in your world? What kind of people are they?
- For your main characters, what have been some of the most compelling moments of their lives?
- What is the setting of your world? Is it all in one biome (ocean, desert, outer space, etc.) or are there multiple locales?
- Are there supernatural forces at work in your world? If so, what are they?
- What supernatural forces are NOT in your world?
- What are the Gods of your world? Are they real beings, or symbolic?
- What stories from ancient mythology (Greek, Roman, Egyptian, Mayan, etc.) are similar to your story (in any way: tone; characters; plot; etc.)?
- What are the rules of your universe?
- What are things that will never happen?
- What are the things that must happen?
- Are there any important objects in this world for a religious, economic, or personal reason to the characters?
- What are the powerful organizations in this world, and how do they run? How do they view each other? How do our main characters view them?
- Who are the people on the Antagonist side that are not all bad? Who is competent? Who is good-hearted? Who has good intentions?

Writing Exercises:

Write the names of 5 myths, or 5 characters from classical mythology that could exist in your story. You don't need to get complicated with it, a bullet-pointed list is perfectly fine.

If you feel inspired, write out a sentence or two about how each myth or character connects with your main story.

If you're having trouble, think of stories that could be the precursors to your story—similar characters who embody the same ideals, or figures that have similar abilities to your main character who they could be related to.

So Long, Farewell, Goodbye

I wish I could tell you that this was the end of your education, and you were ready to write your great masterpiece. I wish I could tell you that this is the ending and you were ready to move on. I wish I could tell you all these endings, but the truth is there is no ending.

Life doesn't have an ending... not mine, and not yours. All it has are chapters, and at the end of each chapter, we're a little bit older, and a little bit more scarred and bruised, but hopefully our bruises have left us a little wiser in the process.

Your education on storytelling will never end. At the ripe old age of 77, a legendary Japanese director said that his best work was still ahead of him, and that he learned by doing, just like you will.

Try and be excellent in just the next five minutes, and if you're not, you'll have 5 minutes after that to try again, and 5 minutes after that, and 5 minutes after that. Don't force it or rush past this moment or compare yourself to some arbitrary or pointless standard set by others.

So now I say to you, "Go."

Don't just sit there waiting to find your voice, or waiting for someone to lift you up onto your journey. Go and start something: write a short story or a poem; join a club; start a business; make something!

It could be as small as a social media account, or as big as a foundation for world peace, but today is the day to change things.

Do it for technology, art, or teenagers in underfunded schools.

But above all, do it for yourself.

Whatever they are, these ideas and experiences that are rattling around in the back of your head are more than just fleeting fancies, they're experiences you'll have that will enrich you as a human being, and you may fail, and you may be betrayed, but you will get back up again, and when you do succeed and hit that home run out of the park, you will make the world a better place because of it.

So go.

They're waiting for you.

Acknowledgments

I want to acknowledge and thank DSTL Arts, and all the wonderful people there who help further the dreams of artists.

Thank you Luis Antonio Pichardo for all your trust, hard work, and wonderful editorial notes. This book would not be as good as it was without your help.

Thank you Angelica Sylvia Castañeda and Abraham Jaramillo for your consistently positive attitude.

Thank you to the fellow members of my cohort, Nikolai Garcia and Mojdeh Amini for your notes and feedback on this book of essays.

I'd also like to thank my many mentors over the years, in no particular order:

- Seth Winston
- Penny Marshall
- Eric Trules
- Ms. Gibson from SHS
- Edward Di Lorenzo
- Harry Cheney
- Duke Underwood
- Robert Ballo
- Ben Hurvitz
- Aja Becher
- Mildred Lewis
- Neema Barnette

- Ryan Harper
- Troy Conrad
- Scott N.
- Sal Santoro
- My middle school Art teacher whose name I can't remember

And thank you to *you*, the reader, for coming on this journey, trusting me, and supporting me.

About the Author

Richard Tucci is an award-winning director, and prodigious producer, who is also multiracial and living with an invisible disability. Mentored by Oscar-winner Seth Winston, and mentored by director, Penny Marshall, he is very honored to have been provided this opportunity by DSTL Arts.

He's also served on producing teams for hit shows on Lifetime, Food Network, and Bravo. Tucci's forthcoming feature film, and feature directorial debut, *Unfriendly Fire*, stars Oscar-nominated actor, Eric Roberts, Golden-Globe nominated actress, Beverly D'Angelo, and comedy legend, Debra Wilson.

You can find him and his team online using @GreaterGrander or at *GreaterAndGrander.com*.

Notes

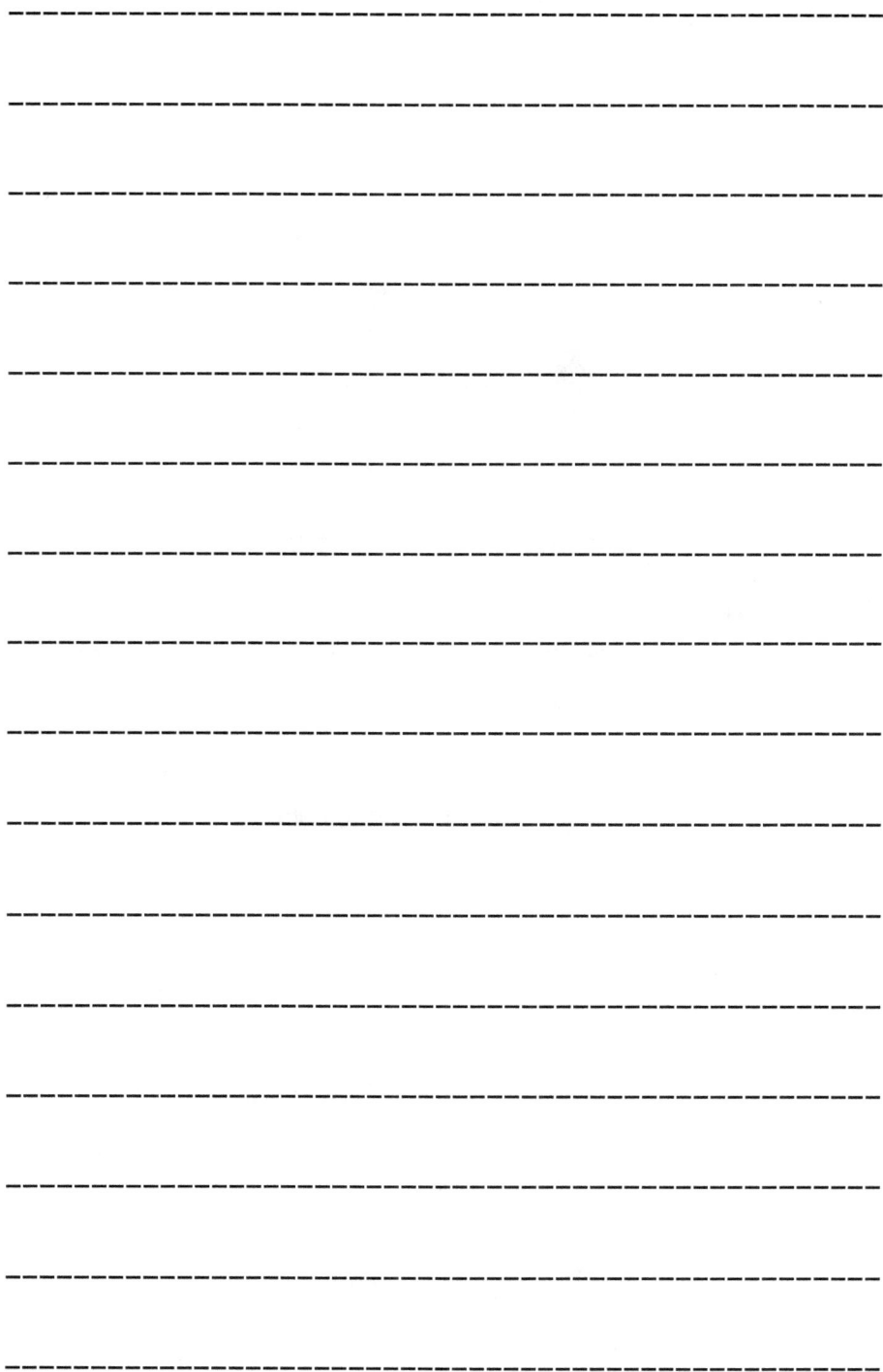

DSTL
arts

This publication was produced by DSTL Arts.

DSTL Arts is a nonprofit arts mentorship organization that inspires, teaches, and hires emerging artists from underserved communities.

To learn more about DSTL Arts, visit online at:

DSTLArts.org
@DSTLArts